A Distant Trumpet
Words of Hope, Courage, and Direction

Sermons by Hugh L. Eichelberger

Edited by Julia Eichelberger

Cover design by Lee Eichelberger
Cover photo by Sara Eichelberger Hutchinson

Editor's Acknowledgments:
Thanks to Carol Ann Davis and Garrett Doherty,
editors of *Crazyhorse* magazine, for generous assistance in formatting.
Thanks to Roy Hutchinson for proofreading help and for many other
acts of kindness during the creation of this book.

To order additional copies, please contact
BookSurge, LLC.
www.booksurge.com
1-866-308-6325
orders@booksurge.com

Behold, I tell you a mystery: We shall not all sleep, but we shall all be changed, in a moment, in the twinkling of an eye, at the last trump: for the trumpet shall sound, and the dead shall be raised incorruptible, and we shall be changed.

I Corinthians 15: 51-52

CONTENTS

Foreword

by Julia Eichelberger

In my childhood in the 1960s, a familiar background noise on Saturdays was the clackety-clack of my father typing a sermon down in the basement. Sometimes he came upstairs to read my mother what he had just written. I remember that she often supplied editorial suggestions, and I think that must have been one of the reasons he wanted try his words out on her. But I can see now that there was something else, too: Dad was writing sermons he needed other people to hear. He didn't capture a static truth on paper; he wrote messages to deliver to other people, and they were not complete until he had a listener. And he knew that he could have no better, wiser listener than my mother. Their collaboration, which I understood only vaguely at the time, interested me intensely. Its importance is clearer to me now: a couple of young, intelligent, idealistic people trying to articulate their ideas about who God was, what the Bible meant, and what calling God had in mind for us, for our church, for our moment in history. Watching these sermons get written, I was learning that the answers to these questions are much too big for any one sermon, that the questions are worth phrasing as beautifully as one can (before Sunday morning comes and we run out of time), and that they come to life when people consider them together, speaking and listening.

These childhood experiences taught me that church was a dynamic exchange, a process in which we were all witness to one another's encounters with God, all fellow sojourners seeking to know what God had in mind for us. Years later, when I had reached the age my parents were in the 1960s, I began teaching at the College of Charleston at about the same time my father came to First (Scots) Presbyterian Church. (He served as senior pastor to this congregation from 1991 until 1996, when he reluctantly took early retirement because of his heart disease.) Once again I was living in the same town where he was writing sermons, and I heard him deliver many of the ones that are in this book. Ten years have passed since then, and I'm glad we have finally gotten these sermons into print, because I think more people need to hear them.

To many people, the Bible is not a window through which we behold a mystery, but a source of absolutist dogma or obsolete myths. The sermons in this book are much more poetic and more profound than that. My father believes that many Biblical images— the wilderness, the empty tomb, the messianic banquet—are not just historical, but also archetypal. They reveal the presence of God in all human experience, a God who is always leading us and giving us new life. These sermons invite listeners to view our own lives through the framework of the great Biblical stories of creation and renewal, exile and wandering, dreams and visions, healing and resurrection. My father preaches that it is possible to trust the Bible, to believe in the power of God's reconciling love, without pretending that our lives and our world are simple or fair. To him, the church is not a source of inflexible rules, but a place for us to acknowledge our need for redemption. As he said on one of those Sundays I heard him preach in the 1990s, the church should function as "a community of moral discourse, where we can wonder together about what God would have us to do and to be." I remember sitting in the sanctuary and hearing him say that; I wished, then, that more people were listening.

I wish now that this book could do justice to the way these sermons sounded. (If you have not heard my father preach, you may wish to visit his blog at http://distanttrumpet.blogspot.com/ to find out how to hear some recordings of his preaching online.) If you ever heard Hugh Eichelberger deliver a sermon, then you will probably recall the cadences of his speaking voice when you read his sentences here, with their combination of lofty language and folksy Southern

8

colloquialisms. Dad's delivery was lyrical and passionate, and it was exciting to hear him address a roomful of people. Individual listeners felt that he was preaching especially to them, yet we knew that at the same time, all around us in the sanctuary, other people were hearing a word for their own lives. Whatever else these sermons said, they always exhorted us to listen, at this moment, to the gospel, for our lives did matter. We could live spiritually or we could live busily oblivious to the spirit at work within us. Anytime we wanted to start listening, we certainly could. No fair saying it was too late for us; no fair claiming we were too weak to live as children of God. These sermons insisted that even in our suffering, even in our sickness and depression and pettiness, God is with us. So don't go thinking God is a nice idea for those who can live up to it; don't go imagining you have no power to live a meaningful life and to make this world more hospitable for all of God's children. No, the preacher told us, there's always something for you to do, today, that will carry you forward on your sacred journey towards the person God has created you to become.

Relentless, that's what Dad's preaching was, and I miss hearing it. I think if you read the sermons in this book, you may find that even now, on the page, his voice still has that urgent quality, seeming to grab readers by the collar and insist on their attention. And if you think he's talking to you, you're right.

The Christian Year

The sermons in this collection are selected from five years of preaching at First (Scots) Presbyterian Church in Charleston, South Carolina. Since the liturgical year and the common lectionary were important in the worship life of that congregation, these sermons are arranged around the great themes of the Christian Year and are based in part on the Biblical selections of the lectionary.

The Christian Year is not something that is prescribed in the New Testament. Rather, it was developed in the church during the fifth and sixth century as a way of keeping time that would be a fitting celebration of the Christian message. It is anchored in the main salvation events that are described in the New Testament. At the time of the development of the Christian Year, few people could read, and the annual observances lifted up in the Christian Year are a recurring memorial of important events in the Christian message.

The Christian Year has not been universally accepted in the church. During the 16th and 17th centuries, Reformers and Puritans protested the Christian Year, fearing that there would be more concern given to the celebration of certain seasons, rather than focusing on the events that the seasons pointed to.

In the past generation, however, many Christians in many traditions have recovered the Christian Year as a way of organizing their common prayer and worship. It has the following seasons: Advent, Christmas, Epiphany, Lent, Easter, Pentecost and Ordinary Time, with colors that assist the worshippers in grasping the significance of the season.

The Christian Year is celebrated in different ways, but the point of all the celebrations is "to keep our eyes fixed on Jesus, the author and perfector of our faith." (Hebrews 12:2)

Introduction

"Lord, we are not worthy, but only speak the word, and we shall be healed."
From the liturgy of the Eucharist

If you are one of those folk who still go to church with any frequency, what do you expect to hear or experience when you go there?

It has been my impression over my thirty-five years as a preacher and pastor that people who come to church on Sunday morning are not quite sure why they are there, or what they should expect. Often they bring with them the frustration of trying to get children dressed in time for church school, or a lingering hangover from too much of something the night before, or some creeping, seeping loneliness or hopelessness that seems always to be leaning against the door of their lives. For many, going to church is like attending a play that they have seen a hundred times before. What has always surprised me is how many keep coming back. If you asked them why, they would most likely respond that it is "the right thing to do" or that church is the place where "I see my friends or can make new friends."

But I believe there is more. Perhaps deep down inside of each of us is the knowledge or the suspicion that there is something here that is worth paying attention to. Something that may assuage the chronic homesickness that is noticed only in strange night dreams, or in some uneasiness that seems to bubble up when things get quiet and still. Is there something here in this place called church and in this book called the Bible that might help make sense of all the nonsense moments of my life, that can sustain one in some personal valley of the shadow? At some level of awareness, I think many suspect there is.

Throughout my ministry people have talked to me about their desire to grow spiritually. I was never quite sure what they meant, and if I asked them, they seemed unsure as well. The thing that preachers often do when someone asks them such a question is to give them a book and suggest they read it. I found that strategy to be unsatisfactory both for them and for me. After much wondering about this desire to grow spiritually, I came up with a definition that suited me and one that I believe is right and true:

To grow spiritually is to pay attention to where God is at work in your life and to respond faithfully to the nudges that come with that presence.

Of course, recognizing and paying attention to where God is at work our lives is not something that most of us have learned to do. And that is where the Bible comes into play.

The Bible is filled with stories of how God has worked in the lives of individuals and groups in the past. These stories can offer us clues about what God's intervention in our lives might look or feel like. The most important stories are archetypal in that they are timeless metaphors that match our experience. While these stories describe something that happened a long time ago, these stories also describe in a profound way events that happen to us all, regardless of our time or place in history. These timeless metaphors are a lens through which to view the particular events of our lives and see how what is happening to us, or not happening, is like the Biblical story.

This led me to see that, if we are to grow spiritually, then we need to know the Biblical stories and know how to connect them to our experiences.

I was trained to be an exegetical preacher, which involves a careful examination of the meaning of the original Biblical text and the original context. When you do this you often end up getting the text down and "breaking its arm." The frequent response of a congregation to this kind of preaching is "Well, that's interesting, but what's the good of it?"

About two-thirds of the way through my ministry I stopped "breaking arms" and started telling stories, and inviting the congregation to wonder with me about how these stories connected to the lives that we were living. I also came to believe that every sermon I preached should be preached first to me, and that if I found it helpful, then there was a good chance someone else might also.

I am indebted in my approach to preaching to Father Herbert O'Driscoll, who taught me that every sermon should include three things: my story, your story, and The Story. The Story is made up of the stories and memories contained in the Bible. It is the story of how God has worked in the lives of groups and individuals throughout history. The great themes of the Bible such as *Journey, Wilderness, Exile,* and *New Life* have a way of showing up over and over again in the stories of every man and woman. It is at the point and moment when an intersection occurs between my story, your story and The Story, that God's word for us is most likely to be heard.

My preaching has also been influenced by the observation that most people, both in the church and out of it, find it hard to make any connection between their story and The Story. The Bible has been taught and understood to be either historical or prescriptive. People who are unable to make any connection between their story and The Story simply quit listening for a word that breaks through the crust that surrounds their lives. It has always been my hope in preaching that the sermon and the liturgy would produce some moment of recognition on the part of both preacher and listener. These are moments when preacher and listener are suddenly caught off guard and say, "My God, that's me!"

That's what these sermons are. It was my hope and intent that in the preaching and hearing these words would help us all to grow spiritually: to develop a greater capacity to see and recognize where God is at work in our lives, and to respond to that in a way that leads to growth and new life.

I am also indebted to Flannery O'Connor, who said in one of her essays, "In every story there are moments of grace that wait to be received or rejected." Such moments are those where there is the possibility for change and new insight. Such moments offer the opportunity to hear the truth that can make one free.

It is my observation that one of the things that seem to be lacking for many today is *Hope.* I was helped in my thinking about this by a little book by James Lynch entitled *Images of Hope*. Lynch says that *Hope* is the ability to imagine a different future.

When I was a small boy, one of the things I did almost every Saturday afternoon was go to what we called then the "picture show," which was usually a double feature. When one of the movies was a western, a common scene was one of settlers journeying across the open prairie, then being ambushed by Indians. Although I now know that this was not a very truthful picture of the settling of the American West and the displacement of Native Americans that occurred in the 19th century, I still recall these scenes fondly because of what happened in them at the moment when all hope seemed lost. Wagons were circled as the settlers desperately tried to save themselves and the enemy moved ever closer. The settlers were suffering many casualties and running out of ammunition. The audience was silent. They saw the end that was coming. And then, suddenly, there would be the sound of a distant trumpet. Cavalry troops were on the way. The settlers would be saved. And the little boys watching the Saturday afternoon double feature stood and cheered.

Consequently, I believe that a major task of preaching in our time is to help folk hear the sound of the distant trumpet that will save them from being overwhelmed by the *facts*, and be energized and sustained by the promises and possibilities that are offered to us by the God who comes to us.

"Once you were no people, but now you are God's people."
1 Peter 2:10a

Advent: A Time of Waiting and Expecting

O come, O come, Emmanuel,
And ransom captive Israel,
Who mourns in lonely exile here
Until the Son of God appear.

"For the whole creation waits with eager longing
for the revealing of the children of God." (Romans 8:19)

I have always thought of Advent as a kind of rehearsal. It is a time when the church community comes together and rehearses what is required of us when we wait upon the Lord with proper expectation. Advent is a time of waiting and expecting. It is a time when we look at the way things are and wonder if that is the way they will always be.

The liturgical year has designated it as a penitential season—a time of self-examination and repentance. The liturgical color is purple, which is the same color as that for Lent. The season of Advent should begin in church with the singing of "O Come, O Come Emmanuel." It is a plaintive hymn of longing sung in a minor key. This ancient chant evokes the sound of monastic longing from centuries ago, and an even earlier memory of a people living in exile and bondage. It recalls a nation carried off into a foreign land as a consequence of their foolishness or as a result of circumstances beyond their control. Something about it resonates with every person living in his or her own personal bondage or exile.

That bondage may be to broken hopes or broken dreams, bodies or relationships that will not heal, despair that clings and saps all vitality, or anything that cuts the nerve of hope and joy and seems beyond the possibility of repair by human hands. This Advent hymn remembers Babylon. It resonates with every person who at some level of awareness knows themselves to be caught in a place from which there seems to be no escape. Advent begins with the bad news of "how it is," and it is with this knowledge that worshipers seek as best they can to sing the Lord's song in a foreign land.

In spite of what many have wanted to make it, Advent is not about getting ready for Christmas as the world defines Christmas. It is not about Christmas decorations and Christmas cookies. It is not a time when we give thanks to God that there is health in the body and money in the bank and that we are not like those poor miserable creatures living in the Third World. Rather, it is about facing the truth about ourselves. There is an "in your face" quality that is central to this liturgical season. Knowing and facing the bad news is the only way to get to the good news. Trying to get to Christmas without Advent is like trying to get to Easter without Good Friday.

Advent begins with the truth about you and me, but swiftly moves to remember the truth about God. Old promises from God are recalled. During the season, those of us who are trapped and surrounded are startled by the sound of a distant trumpet. Help is coming. We have not been forgotten or forsaken. There is hope, and it is hope not based on our own faith, or grit, or determination. It is hope in a God who comes to us in ways that we are unable to control or even anticipate.

Thus, Advent moves from the forlorn hope of the displaced and dispossessed to shouts of joy and celebration. The future will not be constructed from the results of our own past successes or failures. It is a future that comes to us from God. It is *ADVENTUS*.

And when the sound of that distant trumpet is heard, little boys and girls now full grown can stand and shout with joy. And it is because of good news that is both unexpected and undeserved that the liturgical season can find its conclusion on Christmas Eve with the lusty singing of "Joy to the world! The Lord is come. Let earth receive her King; Let every heart prepare him room, and heaven and nature sing."

MIXING MEMORY AND DESIRE

Jeremiah 33:14-16   I Thessalonians 3:9-13   Luke 21: 25-36

In his finest novel, *Look Homeward, Angel,* Thomas Wolfe recalls a time in his life when he seems almost able to remember what had happened even before he was born. He described it this way: "He had been sent from one mystery into another. Somewhere within or without his consciousness he heard a great bell ringing faintly, as if it sounded undersea, and as he listened, the ghost of memory walked through his mind, and for a moment he felt that he had almost recovered what he had lost."

I thought about Thomas Wolfe's quotation as I prepared to begin our celebration of Advent. Of all the seasons of the year, no other causes as much nostalgia and remembering as does Advent and Christmas. There is something about this season of the year that allows—no, perhaps even encourages—the ghost of memory to wander unencumbered through the hallways of our minds.

For many it is a difficult time. It is a time that mixes memory and desire. It is a time when nearly all that we see and hear seems to conspire to open up the walls that stand between the conscious and the unconscious, and to allow forgotten memories to find their way to the surface of our awareness. It is a time when many folk find themselves measuring the distance between the way it used to be and the way it is, or between the way it is and the way it might have been.

We hear the bells of Christmas and we are reminded of other voices from other rooms. The widow is painfully aware of the absence of one who shared many Christmas moments of the past. Parents think of children too soon grown and now so far away. A lonely divorcee thinks of dreams created in happier days and now must deal with the grief of dream unrealized. A single adult living alone wonders if there is some way to get through this season of the year when everyone talks of family and homecoming, and parents now divorced live in separate cities.

It is a time when many people discover the degree to which they are prisoners of the past, when folk discover themselves to be living like exiles in some present moment or place that does not seem to fit and probably never will. It is a time for many when hope is the hardest thing of all to find. For many, this season of the year is a four-week journey into deepening darkness.

The church does not admonish us to deny our hurt, our disappointment, our creeping, seeping hopelessness. Rather, it takes those feelings quite seriously and invites us to go back into the common memory of the community of faith, to listen to another memory. We are invited to listen to the memory of words spoken long ago to a people facing what must have seemed to them a bleak present and a bad future.

To listen to the lessons from the Scripture for today is to stand alongside of other folk in another time. Some of these people had been broken on the rack of national defeat and exile. Others were under persecution, standing alone before the powers and principalities of the time with no army to protect them and no people in high places to plead their case. All the evidence agreed that there was no cause for hope. But the lessons from the Old Testament and the Gospel are both about hope.

The Scripture invites us to go back into the darkness of our common history and hear a word of hope. So it is with this season. It also invites us to go back to some other place and other time and remember not only the hurt and tragedy, but to remember the hope.

Do you remember the hope that you had as a child? Do you remember the hope you took to bed with you on Christmas Eve when you were six? Do you remember the joy of Christmas Day before you had ever heard of separations, sickness, death or failure? Do you remember hope?

The presence of authentic hope is part of what it means to experience the presence of God. Jeremiah was a voice of hope. To a people burned out on life, on themselves and on their fellow men, he said, "Behold the days are coming, says the Lord, when I will fulfill the promise. . ."

Don't give up. Don't give up on yourselves. Don't give up on life or on the future. Don't give up on God. He has not forgotten you.

In a letter addressed to a church that was undergoing persecution, Luke recalls the words of Jesus that spoke of the good and happy ending that God had in mind for all of his children. He tells them that there will be a time when all kinds of calamities will take place. He describes an age not unlike our own, characterized by apocalyptic fear. But the emphasis is not on the problem. Rather, the emphasis is on the solution. The emphasis is on God's happy ending: "When these things begin to happen. . . look up and hold your head high, because your liberation is near at hand."

At Advent, in song, scripture, sermon, and sacrament, we remember days of exile and persecution. We remember oppression and crucifixion. We lay these things alongside the lives that many of us live and are surprised to discover that in some strange way these look like things that have happened in my life and yours. We come and sing a song of people who wondered if God had forgotten them in their exile: "O come, O come Emmanuel, and ransom captive Israel." And as we sing those words, the exile in me longs to be ransomed. That part of my life, which I have sent into some far country, yearns to come home for Christmas. We hear of the birth of a little child and wonder if perhaps the child in me and in you can be reborn, and with it, a rebirth of hope and wonder. We hear about a man broken on a cross who was resurrected by the power of God, and we bring all the things in us that have been broken in some crucifying life experience and wonder if resurrection is possible for us.

As I listen to the memory of the people of God, as I sing the songs and hear the stories, as I taste the bread and the wine, I am aware of something that is like a bell sounding in the depths of the sea. I am aware of that love that will not let me go. I am aware of it because I have felt the love of God in the company of his people. I am aware of it because I have been given surprising moments of grace that helped me see hidden in the face of a stranger one who is really brother or sister—son or daughter—mother or father.

Years ago I preached on Sunday afternoons in a county prison. Services began at 2:00 PM. The guards would call the men to the dining hall. They shuffled in with wrists and ankles constrained by shackles and chains. They would sit down and we would always sing, "Amazing grace, how sweet the sound, that saved a wretch like me. . . ."

A sad picture? Perhaps. But is it not a picture of us all as we come to the table? We come wearing the chains of whatever has happened or failed to happen. We come as prisoners of whatever may bind us. We come just as we are, and we hear again the words spoken long ago to people just back from prison: "Behold, the days are coming, says the Lord, when I will fulfill the promise I made to the house of Israel and to the house of Judah."

On the first day of the Christian year we hear a word about the last day, and are invited to live in the light of that hope and that promise.

To all people in the world who suffer from the creeping sickness of hopelessness—and that probably includes all of us to some degree—the message of Advent is clear. Don't give up hoping. Don't quit on life, on God, on the world, or on yourself. God has not given up on you or forgotten you. Come to this table today and bring with you all the hurt and pain of the years of your life. Bring your loneliness and your despair. Bring your guilt and your anger. Bring it all!

And what is the basis of our hope? It is not our good memories or lack of them. It is not our success, our brilliance or our goodness. It is not grounded on gritty determination or even in saintly faithfulness. The basis of the hope that we hold up and hold onto at Advent is the love, the grace and the faithfulness of God. No matter who you are. No matter how you feel. The good news is that God has not forgotten you or me or those we love. And that memory and that hope is the most important memory and hope of all.

MEMORIES OF THE FUTURE

Isaiah 2:1-5   Romans 13:11-14   Matthew 24:36-44

Did you ever read Charles Dickens' great novel, *A Tale of Two Cities*? In the second paragraph of the first chapter of that novel, Dickens wrote:

> There was a king with a large jaw and a queen with a plain face on the throne of England; there was a king with a large jaw and queen with a fair face on the throne of France. In both countries it was clearer than crystal to the lords of the state, preservers of loaves and fishes, that things in general were settled forever.

According to all the evidence that could be assembled, Dickens tells us, all the significant decisions had been made. Good had been declared good, and wrong had been identified as such. The aristocracy were rich and privileged. The rest of the folk had to scratch for a living. The description that Dickens gave of England and France in the last half of the 18th century was a description of hopelessness. All of the significant indicators suggested that it was "clearer than crystal ... that things in general were settled forever."

Many in our modern world share a similar view of future possibilities. The way things are probably represents the way they will be. Several years ago I talked to a red-eyed, dirty young man who had dropped out of life and who stayed high on drugs. "Why?" I asked him. "Why not?" he responded. Is there any word from the Lord to countless men and women who are struggling with creeping, seeping hopelessness?

Jesuit Priest William Lynch, in his little book *Images of Hope*, tells his reader that an essential ingredient of hope is *imagination*. The capacity to imagine something different from the way it is now is critical to the process of hope. One of the things church should do for me and for you is to keep hope alive. The Word of God, the memory book of the family of faith, can nurture our imagination about what is possible in the future. According to the Bible, things

21

are not settled forever.

The message of Advent is a message of hope because it offers us new possibilities about the world and ourselves. These possibilities are not based on evidence that we can assemble out of our own experience, but are based on the memories of what God has done in the past and what he has promised to do in the future.

Do you remember as a child going to see the movies about settlers and Indians? Those movies were never accurate. They were hard on the Native Americans and always portrayed the settlers in positive terms. But that is not the point I wish to make. What I especially remember was the way in which the climactic moment always came. The wagon train is surrounded. Ammunition is all but exhausted. Victory seems to be in the hands of the enemy. The women and children are doomed. And then it would happen—beyond the distant ridge—the sound of the cavalry's trumpet. I cannot remember a time when that sound was not followed by spontaneous applause from the audience. A new reality is introduced into what had been a hopeless situation. The surprising sound of a distant trumpet—and hope. That is the message of Advent—the surprising sound of God's distant trumpet. Things in general have not been settled forever.

In science and mathematics there is a process called extrapolation. According to the dictionary, extrapolation means to project by inference into an unexplored situation. It is based on the notion that what has been will continue to be in the same way.

How easy it is to live our lives in the light of an extrapolated future. Because it has been, it must continue to be. If my life has been one of disappointment and failure, then it will continue to be. If dishonest politicians have troubled the country then it will continue to be. If my experience suggests that in our family or in my marriage we have never really been able to be intimate, or to solve problems successfully, then that is how it will always be. The danger we face is to believe that somehow things in general are settled forever.

The message of Advent flies in the face of that kind of thinking. To believe in God is to believe in the possibility of change. To believe in God is to believe that things can be different in a positive way. This is the essence of Christian hope.

This morning the word of God invites us to live by a different kind of extrapolation. The word of God invites us to extrapolate a future based, not on what you see, not on the basis of evidence you can gather from your paper or from some personal experience, but based on the memories contained in the Word of God: the memory of Abraham, Moses, Isaiah, John the Baptist, Jesus, the apostles, Paul, the Exodus, the Resurrection, and on a God who says, "Behold, I make all things new."

If you are here today living in the bondage of despair, believing that positive change is neither likely nor possible, then pause with me for a moment and listen to the surprising sound of the distant trumpet of the Advent message. Listen to the good news of the God who can make *all* things—you, your family, your life, First (Scots) Church, Charleston, the world—who can make all things new.

Listen to the word of God brought long ago by Isaiah to a people struggling with despair and surrounded by evidence that suggested that life was going from bad to worse. "It shall come to pass in the latter days that the mountain of the house of the Lord shall be established as the highest of the mountains and shall be raised above the hills. . . They shall beat their swords into plowshares and their spears into pruning hooks; nation shall not lift up sword against nation, neither shall they learn war any more." The way things are is not the way they will always be.

Writing to the church at Rome—to a people who could have easily concluded that the church of Jesus Christ had no future—Paul said, "Salvation is nearer to us now than when we first believed; the night is far gone, the day is at hand. Let us cast off the works of darkness and put on the armor of light." The way things are is not the way they will always be. In the gospel of Matthew our Lord Jesus Christ told His followers that they should live lives of expectancy for God's intervention into history: "Watch, therefore, for you do not know on what day your Lord is coming. . .The Son of Man is coming at an hour you do not expect." The way things are is not the way they will always be.

It is not for you or for me to say the final word about ourselves or about others. In the future that God has promised, men

23

and women "will come from north and south and east and west and sit at table in the Kingdom of God." We may not always recognize those who are citizens of the kingdom or members of the household of faith. God's guest list is quite different than one that we might extrapolate from looking at the evidence of worldly success and importance. In God's economy the last will be first and those who have no credentials will be seated at the head table.

When we listen to the stories in the Bible, we begin to hear the surprising, distant trumpet sound. God's distant trumpet is heard on Easter morning and on a dark hillside near Bethlehem. It is heard in the sound of slave feet trudging out of Egypt. Of people led by the vision of one of God's trumpeters named Moses, who came out of the wilderness and said that slaves don't always remain slaves. It is heard in the sound of water being splashed on the head of a baby who is being baptized. It is heard in the sound of bread being broken and wine being poured out and words spoken that say, "I care, I forgive, I love."

The danger we face is not of having no hope, but of having a hope that is too small. This hope often grows out of a love that hopes for too little and settles for that. Do you remember the story of Helen Keller? Helen Keller was for all practical purposes hopeless. She could neither see nor hear. Her parents considered placing her in an institution that would provide custodial care of the most minimal nature. But before this happened, her parents secured for Helen Keller a teacher whose name was Ann Sullivan. Ms. Sullivan found that the most difficult barrier she had to cross in dealing with Helen was the love of Helen's parents. They were willing to settle for a daughter who could sit at the table and keep herself clean, and that was all. Helen Keller became a great and gifted woman because Ms. Sullivan wouldn't settle for such a limited vision. She believed that Helen Keller was a gifted person and she was committed to reaching her. For Helen Keller, Ann Sullivan was one of God's trumpet players who saw beyond the evidence and called forth the best in her student.

The world needs more trumpeters and dreamers. We already have far too many folk who cannot see beyond the evident and whose contribution is to play a dirge of hopelessness for themselves and for others.

God's word for me and for you is this: listen to hear God's dream for you and dream it along with him. Have you settled for the way things are in your family and given up on yourself and on other people? Have we settled for too little in this church and in our community? Do we believe in our hearts that things in general have been settled forever? If we do, then we do not believe in Christmas.

One of my favorite cartoons shows two prisoners in a cell. They are hanging by chains that are attached to their wrists in a room that has no doors. There is only a small window far above them that is too small to allow either one to pass through. One prisoner turns to the other and says, "Now, here is my plan." At Advent God says to you and to me, "Now, here is my plan!"

When we hope and dream and imagine and look beyond the evidence and remember the Red Sea, Bethlehem, Easter, and our baptism, then we are much more likely to be in touch with God's hope. This hope is based not on the evidence, but it is based on the God who has made himself known to use in the person of Jesus Christ at Christmas.

WAITING FOR CHURCH

Malachi 3:1-4   Philippians 1:3-11   Luke 3:1-6

Much of the Bible is about waiting. A slave people wait in Egypt for deliverance. A people wandering in the wilderness wait for the time when they will enter the Promised Land. Exiles wait to come home. Individuals wait for God to speak a word to them. A captive people wait for the Messiah to come. Over and over again we hear about people who are living their lives in the gap between the way it was and the way it is supposed to be. Over and over again we hear about people who are waiting.

Advent is about waiting. It is a time when we practice what it means to wait upon the Lord. We rehearse what waiting feels like, what it requires of us, what we should be expecting. It is a rehearsal for those moments of grace when Christ will make himself known in the midst of our lives. We are waiting for those moments when we hear the word of the Lord in our ear. We are waiting for those moments when Christ is born in our lives and grace is revealed in a fresh way.

One way of putting this is to say that we are waiting "for church." I am not suggesting that we are waiting for the eleven o'clock hour on Sunday morning to arrive. Rather, I am suggesting that we are looking for and anticipating those moments in our lives when all the things we say and do in church actually are experienced.

Caroline Hughes, a senior consultant with the Alban Institute in Washington, D. C., writes about a conversation that she had with the pastor of a small congregation in a small town. She asked this pastor, Bob, to share with her those times when what he thought church could and should be actually happening in his parish. He said that church happened when people were nurtured and cared about and when Christ was mediated through this nurture and caring. To illustrate he told this story about a family in his congregation. "Alice's first husband had committed suicide, and she raised her children alone. Then she met and married Jim, a big robust man in his sixties who liked engaging in strenuous labor, especially at his lake house. But Jim developed diabetes and lost a leg and couldn't work around his home any longer. He began to talk of suicide and Alice was terrified. The congregation responded. They took Alice out to break her routine of caring for Jim while others spent time with him. His condition grew worse. He began to talk more and more of the lake house he would never see again. A member of the congregation sensitive to the meaning of places in the lives of people offered to take Jim to the lake house and spend the night there with him. They went to the lake house. They sat on the front porch of the cottage for hours. They sat mostly in silence. They talked a little about fishing. At last Jim spoke of dying and of being afraid. Then he blurted out to the other man: 'I love you!' and they cried together." And after that Jim was ready to go back home again. He died six weeks later.

Pastor Bob believed that the reality of the church was experienced on a quiet porch before a lake when a dying man told a friend of his fear. "Church" happened when Jim shared his grief and found the courage to go back home and live the remaining days of his life.

In that place and in that moment, what we talk about and pray about in our formal worship services actually took place. There were no clergy present. There were no religious symbols or rituals, but there was in this event a moment of grace when one human being heard the hopes and fears of another, and grace and community were experienced.

Can you think of such a moment in your own life?

I remember the day I left home to go to college. My father came into my room just before I left. He put his arms around me and kissed me. He prayed that God would watch over me and care for me. And then he let me go. . . and all the things that I had heard about and sung about in church seemed to happen, in that moment of grace.

The reality of the church is experienced when the word of God is really heard and the grace of God truly experienced. It happens when we experience the fulfillment of the promise that says, "Where two or three are gathered together in my name, there I will be in the midst of them."

There is a spiritual that begins with the words, "Every time I feel the spirit moving in my heart I pray." I experience the reality of the church when I experience the reality of the spirit of God. I am moved by those moments. They are special moments when God is near. Change is possible. The child in you that may be a prisoner of your childhood is liberated and peace on earth is experienced.

The lesson from the gospel of Luke tells about a moment when a waiting people heard in a surprising way the word of the Lord. This lesson offers us a clue about what we should expect.

Look again with me at the 3rd chapter of Luke. It looks as if Luke meant to begin his gospel with this chapter. I do not know. I do know that the juxtaposition is startling. Luke begins by cataloging all the people who are in charge of all the life-shaping institutions of his day. The powers and principalities of church and state are in place with their designated leaders. The definitions of good and evil, acceptable and unacceptable, have all been worked out.

But it is not in the midst of these ordered places that the word of the Lord is given, announced, and first heard. Luke tells us that the word of God came to John in the wilderness. It was a word that called for repentance and forgiveness. It was a word that prepared the way of the Lord and made the rough ways smooth and the crooked ways straight. The word was given to and through one who was willing to be still and listen. The word that was given to and through John was a word that challenged the authority of the powers and principalities of the age. It also challenges the powers and principalities that rule within our lives.

The spirit that we wait for is a spirit that challenges the spirit of hopelessness that infects the lives of so many today. It challenges the spirit of resignation that says that the way it is, is the only way it can be. This spirit of God that we wait for is always a threat to the existing order out there and to the existing order in here. It is a spirit that is in this world, but is not of this world. It is a spirit that challenges all oppressive regimes. It challenges the oppression of communism and totalitarianism, but it also challenges all inner totalitarianism. It challenges the inner demons that thwart our creative impulses and undermine our hope about the future.

There is the totalitarianism of old age that says because you are a certain age there is no more future for you. There is the totalitarianism of sexism that says that because you are male or female you must live your life in terms of some previously defined role. There is the oppression of some hurting memory or broken dream that cuts the nerve of your courage and keeps you from venturing out into the unknown.

The spirit that we wait for, the spirit that was given to the church on that day of Pentecost when "church" first happened, is a spirit that can make all things new. It is a spirit that can even renew you and me.

Erik Erikson talks about the struggle that goes on in later life between generativity and stagnation. Do we use our energy to nurture that which is coming into being, or will energy be burned up by people warming themselves around the campfires of remorseful nostalgia?

The spirit of God that came to John, and the spirit that we wait for, is a spirit of generativity. It brooded over the waters and brought order out of chaos. It makes all things new.

Getting ready for Christmas means rehearsing what it means to wait expectantly upon the Lord. It means looking forward to those moments of grace when the presence of Christ is made real in our lives. It means listening for that word which may come in some wilderness moment or place. It means that we look for those moments in life that look like what we talk about, sing about, remember and hope for in the church.

The world tells me that the secret of happiness is low expectations. The world would have you avoid excessive expectation. But that is precisely the opposite of what Advent calls us to do. We are called to wait with joyful anticipation for those moments when Christ is born in our lives. We wait for some lonely hillside moment when some unexpected angel will sing in the darkness of our dreams and tell us that Christ is born, and we are invited to rouse ourselves and go and see this thing that has come to pass, which the Lord has made known to us.

This week I received a letter from a friend who has been through some difficult times. The friend knew of some of the difficult days we have passed through as a church. She wrote: "Don't worry—Jesus is coming back!" And just for a moment church happened and Christmas happened.

Long ago God chose men and women to be messengers of his word. He chooses them to be carriers of his love. No matter who you are or what you may have done or failed to do, God can use you as a messenger of his hope and a bearer of his promise. You can be an instrument of his peace and grace. He can use you and me and this church to be a place and a people where Christmas happens—where the Lord is born afresh—where hope is restored, joy is renewed, hurt is healed. At Advent we hear the promise of the future, but are reminded of the promise of the prophet long ago who said, "Those who wait upon the Lord will renew their strength, they will mount up with wings as eagles, they will run and not be weary."

The message of Advent calls upon us to believe the possibility and to wait upon it with eager joy.

IMAGES OF HOPE—AN UNLIKELY MESSIAH

Isaiah 35:1-6, 10   Matthew 11:2-11

Have you ever found yourself in some prison of circumstances and when you cried out to God, you got no answer? The only sound you heard was the sound of silence. You probably have been there. You may even be in such a place now. If so, then this story—of the question John commissioned his disciples to take to Jesus—might resonate in a remarkable way with your own experience. I know it does with mine.

It probably would have been interesting to hear the conversation of John's disciples before they found Jesus and asked him the question that John had given them to ask.

"Are you the one who is to come, or do we look for another?"

Where you place the emphasis makes all the difference in how you understand the meaning of this question. More times than not we read this question as one of faith and hope. Yet, the more times I have examined this passage, the more convinced I am that when asked by John's disciples, it had become not a question of hope, but a question of disbelief, with more than a hint of sarcasm.

We can be sure that John's disciples were devoted to him. Now, with him in prison, they were not only deprived of their leader and teacher, but their commitment to him was in danger of being discredited. We do not have any way of knowing what they may have talked about on the way to ask the question John had given them, but it may have been that they too had begun to question whether this Galilean could be the long-awaited Messiah. This itinerant rabbi with a rag-tag collection of followers did not look like any Messiah they had ever imagined. Even in his own hometown of Nazareth, they had tried to kill him after he preached in their synagogue. John had gotten into all the trouble he was in partly because of him. Now John wanted to know if it was worth it. Did not the prophet Isaiah say that the Messiah would liberate the prisoner? John had been in the belly of that prison for a long time and longed to be liberated.

31

Why doesn't Jesus do something? The time is now. Could it be that Jesus was just another in a long line of imposters? Look at him. Not much to look at. And look at that crowd of followers he has gathered together. But still, there were the miracles. Maybe those were just coincidental or the result of exaggerated rumors. . . . And so with frustration and disbelief gnawing at them, the disciples of John find Jesus and press him for an answer.

"Are you the one who is to come, or do we look for another?" Surely, not you, but are you the one? Yes or no?

Do you suppose it might have been like that? Was this question asked in a spirit of incredulity and amazement? It was a question brought to Jesus by men for whom this Jesus had not quite lived up to what they had expected as a Messiah from the God who slew the firstborn of all the Egyptians, the God who dried up the Red Sea, the God who had made the sun stand still. It shouldn't be any great difficulty to get busy and get John out of that dark and dreary prison.

Do you suppose that it could have been with this kind of incredulity and sarcasm that they asked this unlikely Messiah to identify himself? I suspect it may well have been. And if so, then these disciples sound for all the world like you and me when someone we love, or we ourselves, are caught in some situation or circumstance from which there seems no earthly way of escape. In such moments, is it not true that we often decide that liberation is in fact the appropriate response from the God who claims to care and claims to know even the number of the hairs of our head?

And what was his answer to their incredulous question? Imagine with me for a moment the return of those messengers to the captive John.

"What did he say? Is he the one?"

"He said to come and tell you what we saw and heard. The blind recover their sight. The lame walk. Lepers are cleansed. The deaf hear. The dead are raised to life, and blessed is the man who does not find me a stumbling block."

"Yes! Yes! But what about prisoners being released? Is that all? No word about release for prisoners? No word about my release? No personal message for me? Am I to stay here and rot in this stinking prison?"

And then they left him to ponder that strange answer. They left him to die at the hands of the man he preached against. We do not know if John ever understood that the kingdom Jesus proclaimed was different than what he had expected and hoped for. I like to believe that John, like Dietrich Bonhoeffer, who spent the last part of his life in a Nazi prison and was executed on a Nazi gallows, discovered in and through this unlikely Messiah a far more profound liberation. Perhaps John's limited vision was healed. And in that healing he was able to see beyond the bars of the cell that would not yield his freedom, and even in that place he caught a glimpse of the borders of his own true country.

We have all been where John was in some way or another. Trapped in some prison that we have created by our own foolish choices, or even a prison that has come to us because of some act of personal faithfulness, and we have expected to be rescued. Or perhaps, we feel the life we have is too limiting, our calling too small, our family too difficult. Surely the Lord meant for you and for me to be more significant than this. Is my life really to be lived in this little nowhere place and in this little unnoticed piece of history with these people?

Are you the one who is to come, or do we look for another? I pray and I don't get any answer. Or the answers seem to make no sense to me and life does not change.

Can you identify with that? We have been there. Perhaps, we are there even now. Caught in some prison of circumstance, or restricted by financial limitations, or by failing health, or by diminishing options, we long to be set free, or fixed, or healed. We send our messengers, our prayers, and all we get in return are enigmatic answers and the indication that our outward circumstances will not change.

Maybe all the changes we can imagine for ourselves are changes we do not really need. So, is there any word of hope for us

33

who often find the changes we imagine unavailable?

I believe there is hope, and I believe we find some clues to that hope in the Scripture reading for this Sunday in Advent.

The first thing I need to hear in these Scriptures is that Jesus will not necessarily liberate us from our situation. We may discover that true healing and real freedom will come to us in the midst of it.

Recently there was an editorial in the journal *Theology Today* that said, "Life is what happens to you when you are making other plans." We set out on our journeys with our plans and hopes and dreams, and suddenly something happens that we did not anticipate, and everything is changed. The real issue that our lesson for today confronts us with is not how to get back on *our* track and get our plans in gear, but how we can be more in touch with God's plans, and how we can live when we have planned something else.

Brother Joseph was sent out to bring his brothers a message from their father. In a jealous rage they threw him into a pit and then sold him into slavery in Egypt. That was not what Joseph had planned. But Joseph made the best of what had happened, and years later, when he spoke to his brothers who were seeking his forgiveness, he said, "You meant it for evil, but God meant it for good."

Jacob stole his brother's birthright and deceived his father. His brother wanted to kill him and Joseph fled in fear. In a lonely field Jacob lay down to sleep, and in his sleep he had a profound vision about the presence of God. His spiritual blindness was cured and he saw, in a way he had never seen before, that "God is in this place, and I did not even know it."

In every place where some significant growth or insight has taken place in my life, it has come through some interruption, or something I did not expect, or that I longed to be free from. It happened when I was planning something else.

This is the good news we can hear in this lesson for today. Some dry, desert, barren place in your life can be transformed into a place of life and beauty through the power of God. That is what this word from Isaiah is really about.

The Bethlehem event reminds us that Jesus is coming, ready or not. This unlikely Messiah may meet us at the office, or in a stranger at the mall, or in a dream that comes to us deep in some nighttime moment and place.

This Advent message invites us to pay attention and to keep on praying and hoping and struggling. Never, ever give up.

Send your messengers to Jesus. Ask your incredulous questions. Wonder why he doesn't do what you want him to do. But just when you think he has forgotten you or doesn't even care, he will come to you in some unlikely and unexpected way, and you will see something you have never seen before.

He is coming—ready or not!

My prayer for you is that something crippled in you will be healed, some blindness cured, some dead place restored to life. When that happens we can know the real liberation that comes when we realize that everything does make sense, because everything is in the hands of God.

This is our glory and our hope. The sounds that we hear, if we listen carefully, are the sounds of excitement and gladness and laughter that float through the air from a great banquet.

And we will give You all the praise and all the glory, world without end. In the name of Jesus who has come, and who will come again.

GOD WITH US

Isaiah 7: 10 – 16   Matthew 1: 18 - 25

What is life like for you on Christmas Eve, 1995? Do you believe that the way it has been is the way it always must be?

What kind of Biblical metaphor would you use to describe where you are today? What story in the Bible looks or feels like your life today? There are many important stories in the Bible that have helped me and others to describe what is going on in my life and theirs. An early story in the Bible is the story of Abraham, who was called by God to go on a journey, and he went out on that journey not knowing where he was to go. There is the story of Jacob wrestling with an angel by the riverbank in the night, trying to come to terms with who he was going to be and what he was going to do with his life. One of the earliest stories in the Bible is the story of the children of Israel living in slavery in Egypt. Their lives were under the dominion and rule of a Pharaoh who was demanding more of them than they could do, and all the evidence seemed to say there was no hope. Then there is the story of their miraculous deliverance—but it was deliverance that led them into the wilderness, where they wandered for forty years, never quite sure how long they would be there. Then there was Babylon. A land where the people of God were taken as a result of their disobedience, leaving behind the broken pieces of their nation and their hope. The New Testament begins with God's people living their lives under the domination and rule of the Roman Empire, hoping and praying for the Messiah who had been promised long ago.

What do all of these stories have in common? The common element is a crisis. It is a crisis that cannot be resolved by human efforts. It requires the intervention of something from outside. In the Bible, that something is the God who comes with new hope and new possibility. It is not just any god but a God who tells a man named Moses that his name is "I Am"—the first person singular denoting continuing personal action. It is a God who tells Isaiah that he is to be called "Emmanuel," which means "God with us." The message of the Bible is that no matter who you are, no matter what you have done or failed to do, you are not alone or abandoned, no matter what the evidence may say. The way it is, is not the way it must always be.

What about you on this Christmas Eve in 1995? Do you find yourself living in the promised land of hopes fulfilled and of dreams that have come true? Does your God seem to be in his heaven, and is all right with your world? If that is so, then you should count yourself among the fortunate.

There are many for whom that is not true. Perhaps you have come here today with some vague sense that God has called you to leave something behind and go on a journey, but you are not sure where to go or where God is. Perhaps you find yourself living in some personal Egypt where you have been laboring for years, trying to fix something or somebody that will not be fixed, and you wonder if there will ever be any deliverance from your land of bondage. Are you wrestling with some crisis in your life, seeking to discover what your real name is and who you will be in all of your tomorrows?

Are you living in a wilderness of change brought on by a broken promise, or a broken body, or a broken dream? Or perhaps all the choices and decisions of your past have led you to some personal Babylon, and you teeter on the verge of losing hope. Are you living in bondage to a grief that will not heal or a memory too painful to speak? There are many folk for whom Christmas is hard. It brings into sharp focus the gulf between how it might have been or should have been, and how it is.

Certainly there is much for all of us to be thankful for. For most of us there will be warmth in our homes, food on the table, presents under the tree, and money in the bank. For most of us the troubles that many in the world will experience on Christmas Day are as far from us as Bosnia, or as remote as a homeless shelter on Christmas Eve. Therefore, let us not engage in an orgy of self-pity or become so self-absorbed that we lose sight of all the blessings that we have been given. Let us not lose sight of the fact that no matter how lonely we may feel, we are here today because others have loved us and stood by us. Let us not lose sight of the fact that no matter how impoverished we may feel, by all standards we are greatly blessed and have much to be thankful for and to celebrate in this holy season. But on the other hand, let us never say to ourselves or to those around

37

us, "You should not feel what you are feeling or think what you are thinking." Rather, let us honor whatever feelings we have, and not deny the lonely or hurting child within us with platitudes and easy words.

Let us instead, like the shepherds of long ago, go and see this thing that has come to pass that the Lord has made known to us. Let us ask about the meaning of Christmas and be curious about the corning of a God who says his name is Emmanuel, God with us. Let us do this in order that we will not miss Christmas, and it will not miss us.

Christmas is the memory of a God who breaks the laws of nature and of science and offers us something entirely new and unexpected. It is the memory and proclamation of a God who is with us, for us, and has come to intervene in the natural order of things.

The second law of thermodynamics is that the entropy of an isolated system always increases. Entropy, according to the dictionary, is disorder, chaos, and randomness. In an isolated system, the disorder, chaos and randomness always increase.

It must have been an overpowering sense of this entropy that led William Butler Yeats to write in his poem, "The Second Coming,"

Turning and turning in the widening gyre,
The falcon cannot hear the falconer;
Things fall apart; the center cannot hold;
Mere anarchy is loosed upon the world. . .

Left to our own resources, things fall apart. Randomness, chaos, and disorder increase. We become like the falcon that cannot hear the falconer. Anarchy is loosed upon the earth. Entropy increases. The good news of Christmas is that something entirely new has been added. God breaks the second law of thermodynamics. A light shines in the darkness and the darkness of entropy does not overcome it. The word becomes flesh and dwells among us, full of grace and truth. Unto us a child is born.

And what is the meaning of this birthing? What is the significance of this child? The birth of Jesus is the birth of new hope and of new possibility. The child that is born is Emmanuel, God with

38

us. And the danger that we face at Christmas and on every day of the year is the danger of believing that the way it is, is the only way it will ever be. It is the danger of believing that I must spend all of my days in Egypt and live out my life in Babylon. It is the danger of believing that Pharaoh is more powerful than God and that Nebuchadnezzar is the Lord of life. For God to break the laws of science and of history is a frightening thing. It flies in the face of logic, of experience, and of all that has been taught us by the wisdom of the world. Joseph was afraid when an angel said to him that the child conceived in Mary was of the Holy Spirit, and that she would bear a son and call his name Jesus, and that Jesus would save his people from their sins. Jesus would save his people from entropy—from chaos, disorder, and randomness.

In W. H. Auden's poem *Christmas Oratorio*, he records an imaginary conversation between Joseph and the angel. Joseph says that he wants one irrefutable piece of evidence that what the angel says is true. The angel responds, "No, you must believe." And that is the way it always is. We hear the message, and it goes against everything we have learned from observation and experience. The presence of this new possibility is frightening and disturbing. Is it true? Is there one piece of irrefutable evidence that we can find? No! We must believe. Or we refuse to believe, and chaos, disorder, and randomness continue.

The birth of this baby reminds us that hope and new possibility are always fragile things. They need to be nurtured and cared for. They need to be held and caressed. Perhaps you are here today like Mary must have been long ago, feeling some spiritual morning sickness, because there is something within you that is small, alive, and growing.

Are you pregnant with God and with new possibility? Is that which you find within you of the Holy Spirit? Then what do you do? Do you provide the care and nurture that the fragile presence demands, or do you abort the hope and the new possibility? Do you decide for entropy and decide against God? In Luke's gospel, he tells of shepherds watching their sheep at night and of the disturbing appearance of angels to announce the birth. Luke tells us that they were afraid. And so are we afraid, when something new and unexpected is given to us. The shepherds could have run away. They could have ignored the message and the messengers. But they did none of these

39

things. They did what we should do. They said one to another, "Let us go and see this thing that has come to pass, that the Lord has made known to us." And they went on their way to Bethlehem, and there they found Mary and Joseph and the baby Jesus lying in a manger.

For those today who are living in some personal Egypt of bondage, or in an exile place that is far from home, or wandering in a wilderness of confusion and uncertainty—for those who believe that the way it is and the way it has been is the way it will always be, the good news of Christmas is the news of new hope and new possibility. For unto us a child is born; unto us a son is given. Where is Christmas happening for you today?

It happens when something breaks into our lives that was totally unexpected and brings with it the opportunity for joy and new life. Christmas is finding what you have been looking for all of your life, when you did not even know that you were looking for it. Christmas is a gift. It turns everything upside down and leaves us breathless with joy and anticipation. Christmas happens when suddenly and without warning you are given a gift that makes all things new. The way it has been is not the way it must always be. But in order to receive the gift we must be willing to act with faith. We must be willing to let go of the past and take hold of the new possibility that is given to us by a God who is with us, and for us, and not against us.

So what will it be? Will we be like the innkeeper who told Mary and Joseph there was no room for them? Will we be like Herod who sought to destroy the child because he threatened the way things were and always had been? Will we be like the citizens of Bethlehem who didn't even notice that something incredible was happening in their midst? Or will we be like the shepherds who responded with faith to an irrational presence that came to them in the night, who said, "Let us go to Bethlehem and see this thing that has come to pass, which the Lord has made known to us." The choice is yours, and it is mine. We can live in Egypt, or in exile, or wander forever in some wilderness of confusion and despair. We can believe that disorder, and chaos, and randomness are here to stay, and Christmas will come and go and nothing will have changed. Or we can be wise men and women and follow the star that leads to new life, to new hope, to new possibility. And forever after, everything will be new and different.
40

Christmas: The Birth of Hope

What child is this who, laid to rest
On Mary's lap, is sleeping?
Whom angels greet with anthems sweet
While shepherds watch are keeping?

If Advent represented the preface to The Story, then Christmas is the first chapter. There is no single word that captures the meaning of this season. It is enigmatic, paradoxical, and unfathomable. It has a way of measuring the distance between how it is and how we would like for it to be. Through the years we have done all we can to domesticate the season and reduce it to something sweet and simple. But all of our efforts simply testify to the fact that this is a time where our spiritual amnesia is demonstrated more completely than in any other season of the year. We know that it is important, but are often not quite sure why. It is as if we can't quite remember what it is really about, but know it is about something terribly important and deserving of great celebration.

The story that is remembered and retold each year is one that raises far more questions than it provides answers. It is about birth. It is about new possibility. It is about a gift that is given in the most unlikely way and place. Of all the people that show up in the Christmas story, the one who seems to understand it best is Herod. Herod saw it as an assault upon the powers and principalities of the world. It was the beginning of an apocalyptic struggle between the forces of Good and the forces of Evil.

If one accepts the view that the Bible offers us clues about how God acts in history, then the Christmas event shows us things about God that we would never have expected. It provides us with hints about how and where God is likely to show up in our lives.

God often comes, not in places where we would look for him, but precisely in those places which seem devoid of possibility and hope. All that is necessary to see this is to look at the main players in this surprising story of two young people having to deliver their firstborn child in what was little more than a stable out back of an inn where they could find no room. If we are to believe that the baby that is born is God incarnate, then the story tells us about God's willingness to entrust his presence to the poor and to the powerless. It tells us that the first signs of God's presence are often as fragile as a fetus. It reminds us that the birth of God then, and the birth of God in each of us, is always the birth of possibility and hope. Mary and Joseph, two poor and insignificant young people, were given the responsibility to care for the child that would forever change the course of history. They did not understand what was happening, but they were trying to do the right thing and care for the frail baby born to them in a nowhere place and time.

Therefore, this season calls us to pay attention. Pay attention to spiritual morning sickness. Believe that the God who was incarnate in Jesus desires to be born in you and in me. Look for the presence in our own Bethlehem places when we feel that all logical reasons for new hope have run their course. The birthing will not be easy and the place may not be comfortable, but in some night time moment of life when we have been displaced by the powers and principalities of the world God often shows up and makes all things new.

Unto us a child is born. Unto us a son is given, and his name shall be called Emmanuel, God with us.

> *This, this is Christ the King,*
> *Whom shepherds guard and angels sing;*
> *Haste, haste to bring Him laud,*
> *The babe, the son of Mary!*

THE BIRTH OF GOD

Isaiah 9:2-7   Titus 2:11-14   Luke 2:1-20

We have gathered here today in this special place to celebrate a memory, a present reality and a hope. The mood of our celebration has already been established in the singing of our opening hymn.

"O come, all ye faithful, Joyful and triumphant, O come ye, O come ye to Bethlehem!"

It is, therefore, with a spirit of triumphant joy that we are invited to go again to Bethlehem and see this thing that has come to pass that the Lord has made known to us. Through the memory preserved in scripture and in song, we go to the little town of Bethlehem and make our way to a manger behind an inn. There we find a poor peasant family and a newborn child wrapped in swaddling clothes and lying in a manger. We have been told, however, that this is not just any baby. This is a very special child. This is Emmanuel—God with us. This is the child whose birth has been foretold by the prophets and who represents the fulfillment of a promise. Luke has told us in his gospel that this is no natural event. Rather, this child's birth is a result of an act of God. This child has no human father in any biological sense. He is born of a virgin. But that is not all that is peculiar about this particular birth. According to the gospel of John, the Word has become flesh in the birth of this small child. We have come to Bethlehem to celebrate the Birth of God.

That fact is often missed in all the carols and gatherings of Christmas. In the midst of "Silent Night" and "Here Comes Santa Claus," we often fail to reflect on the incredible message of the Christmas event. God has entered the womb of a woman. He has taken the form of a fetus. He has entrusted himself to the care and nurture of a young and inexperienced couple who seem almost devoid of earthly resources. It is, for God, a real emptying. In the womb he is waiting and is helpless. In this act he has become like us, who often are waiting and helpless.

Of all the memories and messages that the church celebrates and proclaims to the world, this is one of the most powerful. For in it we see the work of an incredibly trusting God who, in a great act of love, became flesh and dwelt among us. It would be less surprising if God had simply appeared among us as a grown man and in that form went about doing good. But he does not. Rather, he chooses to share in the fullness of all humanity from conception to death. God was born in and through a mortal woman. The Word became flesh and dwelt among us.

We celebrate that memory today and all of the love and trust that is implicit there. It must not, however, go unnoticed that the event has metaphorical dimensions. It should remind each of us of a truth that was first uttered by St. Francis of Assisi, who wrote that each person, like Mary, is pregnant with the Lord, struggling to give him birth. The God who was born at Bethlehem long ago, who became flesh and dwelt among us, is the same God who comes to us and seeks to be born in our lives. The first signs of his presence are often as fragile and easily missed as the first signs of life that a woman might feel in the early weeks of pregnancy. Each person is a womb for God. We are all filled with the potential of becoming a vessel of the living God.

Therefore, while we have come here to celebrate the memory of the birth of God at Bethlehem, we are also here to celebrate the good news that each of us can receive the Lord in our lives through the overshadowing of the Holy Spirit. Bethlehem not only happened a long time ago, it might be taking place in your life this very day. It may be taking place in the life of someone near you. Our vocation is to help each person give birth to the God that seeks to be born in every man and in every woman. We are here today to celebrate the present reality of Christmas. We celebrate Emmanuel—God with us.

But we also celebrate the hope that is revealed in the birth, life, death and resurrection of our Lord Jesus Christ. His life among us is truly an aberration. In it we see signs and hints of the kingdom that is to come. In his life the future collapses in upon the present and the way it will be in the time that is to come is revealed in his life, in his actions and in his resurrection.

For many, Christmas is a time of mixed feelings. There is no other time of the year when we are more painfully aware of the relationships that have been severed by death. Christmas can easily be a time where many have a heightened sense of painful impoverishment. But a true celebration of Christmas will help us break free of that prison of sadness. A true celebration of this day will help us maintain the joy with which we gathered and the triumphant expectation with which we can move into the future.

The celebration of the Eucharist reminds us that the one whose birth we celebrate today is also the one who is among us and the one who will greet us in the future. As we come and gather round this holy table on this holy day, we can be assured that we are not alone. We break this bread and drink this cup not only with the Lord of life, but we gather around this table with "all the saints who from their labors rest." As I come to this table I can celebrate this special Christmas feast, which foretells of that future time when we will all be home for Christmas. But for today is it is enough to know that gathered at this table with me and with you are all the saints of all the years. My Aunt Loulie is here. My friend Bob is here. My mother and my father are here. At this table where Christ is the host, we are all home for Christmas, and everyone is accounted for.

O come, all ye faithful, Joyful and triumphant, O come ye, O come ye to Bethlehem!

Epiphany: Breaking Open The Covenant

In the liturgical year it does not take long to get right to the point. This Word made flesh, this one whose name is Emmanuel, the child born of a virgin, is not just a savior come to save the Jews. The light that led wise men to Bethlehem is a revelatory event that makes it clear that this Jesus is for all men and women.

A number of years ago I heard a Jewish theologian say that the thing that was offensive to the Jews about Jesus was that he broke open the covenant. Jesus announced that God's love is broader and deeper and wider than anyone had ever imagined. Of course, that was the point that Jesus was making when he preached his famous hometown sermon back in Nazareth.

Epiphany means manifestation. This is not a limited word to a limited few. It is good news for all men and women regardless of their race, or national origin, or sexual orientation, or anything else.

WISE MEN AND THE SACRED CHILD

EPIPHANY SUNDAY
Isaiah 60:1-6   Ephesians 3:1-12   Matthew 2:1-12

Do you remember the 1980 Presidential debate between Mr. Carter and Mr. Reagan? The only line most folk remember is the well-known quip of Mr. Reagan in response to something Mr. Carter said. "There you go again, Mr. President." That statement came back to me as I read the lessons for today. I found myself wanting to talk back to the scriptures and say, "There you go again—talking about a journey."

Have you ever noticed how frequently the Bible talks about and describes people involved in some kind of journey? The first word that God speaks to Abraham is an invitation to go on a journey: "Go from your country and your kindred and your father's house to the land that I will show you." It is in the midst of his journey that God
46

meets Jacob and gives him a new name. God speaks to Moses out of a burning bush: "Come, I will send you to Pharaoh that you may bring forth my people, the sons of Israel, out of Egypt." Then there is the story of a people who journey forty years in the wilderness on their way to the Promised Land.

There are other journeys. Some are personal. Some involve a whole nation. There is the journey into exile. The lesson from Isaiah for today is an announcement to those poor, displaced people in Babylon. The prophet announces the good news that they have not been forgotten. They will go on another journey, but this journey will lead home.

The imagery is powerful. Picture, if you will, a decimated city. Jerusalem is a poor place. You are one of the few folk who managed to remain. There seems to be no future for this place or for Israel. Poverty is everywhere. A nation has been abducted. Any thought of political power or influence appears ridiculous. Then everything turns around. One day as you stand on the watchtower, you see great streams of men and women coming from many directions. The exiles are coming home. The city will be restored to its former glory. Yet, it is not only the exiles that journey to Jerusalem. People come from north and south and east and west. Jerusalem, the holy city, is the goal of the journey.

The motif of the journey repeats itself in the lesson from the gospel of Matthew. In his description of the nativity, Matthew tells us that the infant Jesus was visited by wise men from the East. They had come on a long journey in search of the sacred child. They had seen his star in the East. They had come to worship him. The trip surely was not easy. Their travels finally bring them to the holy city, Jerusalem, where they meet Herod.

When Herod is told of the birth of the sacred child who will be a king, he is troubled. He seeks to use the wise men to help him find and destroy this one who appears to be a threat to his power. But the wise men are not deterred. The journey continues. The wise men find the sacred child. They worship him. They offer him the finest gifts they have. They pay attention to their dreams and refuse to be used by Herod to destroy the child whom they have come so far to see.

47

All men and all women are called to go on a journey of faith and of faithfulness. All are called to search diligently for the birth of the sacred child in the world and in the lives of individuals.

This invitation to undertake the journey is to all people. It is extended to those who may be living in an exile imposed by personal sorrow, failure, disappointment, grief, or hostile circumstances. The invitation to come and worship the sacred child is delivered to the rich and to the poor, to the powerful and to the powerless, to the successful and to the failures, to the law-keepers and to the lawbreakers. It is a gracious invitation. No one is excluded. In the course of this journey it shall be revealed that all men and women are brothers and sisters. All are members of the same family and are called to worship the same sacred child. Travelers on this journey will learn that God's justice and mercy exceed any notions we have of justice, and stretch our broadest definition of mercy.

Wise men and wise women in our time will pay attention to unusual signs that challenge them to leave old ways. They will follow leads as unnatural as stars. Wise men and wise women of our time will be willing to undergo great difficulty and pay a great price to reach the place and the moment where the sacred child is being born. That place may be within the world or within the heart of each traveler.

Wise men and women will beware of the forces of Herod that seek to destroy the sacred child and deter us from the journey's goal. These forces may be in the form of a cynicism about life that leads one to give up the journey in despair. The forces of Herod may be an infatuation with material things that tempt even the wisest man to forsake the sacred journey and pursue the goal of wealth and power.

Where is Herod in our time or in our lives? Who is Herod? Herod is the death force. Herod is seen in the love of power at the expense of peace. Herod reveals himself in the temptation to believe that life has no purpose or meaning and is a random series of disconnected and meaningless events. Herod is the temptation to believe, "I am not my brother's keeper."

Matthew tells us that "Jesus was born in the days of Herod the king." Wise men and women know that the sacred child is *always*
48

born in the days of Herod the king. Wise travelers know that the journey that leads to the sacred city and on to the birth of the sacred child will *always* pass through Herod's court. Wise travelers will follow their star and ignore the invitations and resist the traps of all the Herods that are encountered along the way.

On Epiphany the church celebrates the universality of the manifestation of the sacred child. He has come to invite all to go on a journey of faith and faithfulness. We are assembled here today because we have responded to some personal star or voice or hope or dream that has lead us to search for the holy city and the sacred child. At this table we are invited to pause on the way and to be refreshed. Behold, a table is prepared for us in the presence of all the Herods of the earth. Behold, companions to travel with us. Men and women, young and old, rich and poor, sick and well, red, yellow, black, white— all manner of people will come from north and south and east and west and sit at this table in the kingdom of God. Behold, a challenge and an invitation to continue the journey. "Go into all the world and proclaim the gospel." Behold, a promise to take with us on the way. "Lo, I am with you always, even to the end of the age." Behold, a memory that assures us that we need never fear the forces of Herod or Pilate or even death itself. "He is not here; he is risen. . . . Because I live, you will live also."

As wise men and as wise women, let us follow the star. Let us seek the birth of the sacred child. Let us continue the journey.

A New Creation

Genesis 1:1-5   Acts 19:1-7   Mark 1:4-11

Called one of the most celebrated plays of contemporary American life, *Death of A Salesman* by Arthur Miller tells the story of the final days of the life of salesman Willy Loman. The play concludes with his family and friends' response to his accident/suicide. In this play Willy Loman is depicted as a man whose luck and life are running out. Troubled by something he cannot put his finger on, he loses his ability to concentrate on his work. Eventually he loses his hold on everything and in despair ends his life in an automobile crash.

In the last scene of the final act we find Willy's wife, two sons, and a friend, standing beside his grave. The friend tries to say something good about Willy, but one of the sons is determined to tell the truth. He says, "He had the wrong dreams. All, all wrong." The other son does not want to hear a bad word about his father. He cries out, "Don't say that." But his brother will not let it go. "He never knew who he was. . . . .the man didn't know who he was."

The power and appeal of Arthur Miller's play were obviously grounded in the fact that many people who saw it could identify at some level of their lives with the plight of Willy Loman. He was a man trying to make it in the world "on a smile and a shoeshine," a man trying to make it alone, but never really sure who he was or what the goal and purpose of his life was. He never knew who he was. Willy Loman represents a lot of people.

This play by Arthur Miller was written over forty years ago, but the identity question, "Who am I?" is at the root of many people's problems. It has become somewhat of a fixation for modern humanity because many of us have looked in the wrong places for the answer. We have believed what the world has told us about who we are and have defined ourselves as consumers of things and experiences. We have believed the slick ads that have told us that the goal of life is to get more and more, and to be less and less attached to others. The hucksters who tell us that our identity is determined by where we live, the car we drive, the money we make, the degrees we have, or the clothes we wear, have taken us in. This basic question of identity causes much psychological pain among many persons. It is a question that you and I bring with us every time we come to worship.

Not to know your true identity is tragic, but there is no reason for that to be true of anyone who is in the church. You may not always remember who you are. You may not always act like who you are. You may even try to live under the illusion that you are your own person and no one has a claim on you. But if you have been baptized, if you come to church with any frequency and hear what the church says and see what the church does, then the question of who you are is a question that should be answered weekly. William Willimon, in his book *Worship as Pastoral Care*, tells the reader that "to raise the question 'who am I?' is to raise the question that the church should always be impatiently waiting to answer."

The gospel lesson for today recalls the baptism of Jesus. Liturgically, this first Sunday after Epiphany is referred to as The Baptism of the Lord. In the hearing of this story of Jesus' baptism in the Jordan by John the Baptist, we are allowed to stand in the crowd of witnesses who were there long ago and saw this moment that marked the beginning of the public ministry of our Lord. The fact that Jesus, a man who knew no sin and is the Word made flesh, would need or desire to be baptized is a mystery that is never fully explained. It is clear, however, that in this experience Jesus heard a clear word about his own identity. If there was any question in his mind about who he was, that question was answered in his baptism. As he emerges from the water, Mark tells us, a voice came from heaven saying, "Thou art my beloved son; with thee I am well pleased." It was in the moment of his baptism that Jesus heard an unequivocal word about his own identity.

On any Sunday morning the church has many means of speaking to the question of identity that each of us brings to this place. I may be reminded of my true identity in the creed, in a hymn, a prayer, or in participation in the Lord's Supper, but the first and clearest word about my true identity is given to me by the church in the sacrament of baptism.

At the conclusion of a service of baptism—usually when an infant is baptized—the minister will turn to the congregation and say, "Remember your own baptism and be thankful." Today we have witnessed the baptism of our Lord through the words of Mark's gospel. In response to that event I would say again those words that are said at the conclusion of other baptisms: "Remember your own baptism and be thankful." There is no clearer answer given to the question "Who am I?" than the answer given in the sacrament of baptism. The problem that many of us have is that we not only do not remember it—because it was probably done for you when you were very young—but we do not really understand the full significance of that event. Thus, as we remember our own baptism this morning I would like to say two things about its meaning.

First, in baptism we are given a new identity. The central moment in the baptism of an infant takes place when the minister speaks the child's name and then says, "Child of the covenant, I baptize you in the name of the Father, and of the Son, and of the Holy Spirit." Your old name may have been Failure, or Isolated, or Outsider, or Hopeless or No Good. In baptism you are given a new name: Child of the Covenant. This is not something that we earn. It is not something that we deserve. It is a gift. It is something that is done *to* us. God's affirmation of us in baptism is indelible. It is once and for all. This was a great source of comfort for Martin Luther, who suffered at times (as do all of us) from self-doubt and despair. At those low moments, Martin Luther received great comfort by touching his forehead and saying "Baptismatus sum"—"I am baptized."

But we are given more than a private identity. Baptism tells us that we are not only children of God, but we are also members of the household of faith. In the epistle of I Peter we hear the words clearly stated: "Once you were no people, but now you are God's people; once you had not received mercy, but now you have received mercy." In baptism the church is saying to the person baptized: "You must never again think of yourself as on your own. You are ours, and we are God's. As we claim you and as God claims you through us, so also your new brothers and sisters will make claims upon you. You are now part of the body. You are part of that new creation called the church. There is no longer any place for petty divisions. There is no longer any place for nursing grudges. There is no longer any place for people who want to believe that how they live and what they do with their resources is a private matter." One of the great heresies that is abroad in our land is the false idea that you can be a Christian in isolation from other Christians. You cannot be a good Christian

52

and not be a part of some church. You cannot be a faithful disciple of Jesus Christ and isolate yourself from the body of Christ. In baptism we become members of a family. It is in this family of faith that I will fully come to know and discern the will of God for my life and the full implications of my new identity. In baptism I am not told what I ought to be; rather, I am told who I am, and in the church I am encouraged to live in the light of my true identity.

Who am I? Who are you? Who are we? Baptism says it all. In baptism we become a new creation. The old man dies and the new is born. No matter what the world may say about you. No matter what names anyone has ever called you. In those moments when you feel a cold breath of despair on your neck, remember the good news of your baptism. You are a chosen race, a royal priesthood, a holy nation, God's own people, that you may declare the wonderful deeds of him who called you out of darkness into his marvelous light. Remember your own baptism and be thankful!

THE GIFTS OF GOD FOR THE PEOPLE OF GOD

Genesis 1:1-5   Mark 1:4-11

Have you ever felt like giving up on God because you felt that God had given up on you? I have, and I imagine most of you have. There are moments in the life of every person when faith is hard to come by. When God seems to be in his heaven and all seems to be right in the world, it is not hard to believe in a loving and providential God. When there is health in the body, happiness in the home, and money in the bank, it is easy to say "AMEN" to the notion that God numbers the hairs on our head and knows each of us by name. When a failing business suddenly turns around, or when the report from the biopsy comes back and there is no cancer, we can stand in the midst of the congregation and sing with gusto, "Now thank we all our God." But there are other moments when faith in a loving and all-powerful God seems to fly in the face of experience. A child is stricken with an incurable illness; a longed-for baby is lost in the first trimester of pregnancy: a loved one is struck down by an illness that defies the wisdom of modern medicine.

I remember years ago walking out into an apple orchard late on a September afternoon in Western North Carolina and telling a nine-year-old boy that his 33-year-old father was dead from cancer, and that his mother, now pregnant with a fifth child, would be alone. Amidst trees burdened with the unpicked harvest, I did my best to comfort that little boy, and wondered, "If God is God, can he be good? If God is good, can he be God?" The slings and arrows of circumstance and tragedy often seem to make a mockery of all of our theological affirmations.

Even John Calvin perceived plainly the discrepancy between what we say we believe and what happens to us. He wrote, "A blessed resurrection is proclaimed to us—meantime we are surrounded by decay. We are called righteous—and yet sin lives in us. We hear of ineffable blessedness—but meantime we are oppressed here by infinite misery." The late theologian Reinhold Niebuhr spent the first 13 years of his ministry as pastor of Bethel Evangelical Church in Detroit. He chronicled his ministry in a little book entitled *Leaves from the Notebook of a Tamed Cynic*. As he prepared to leave Bethel

Church after 13 years, he wrote in his book, "It is almost impossible to be sane and be Christian at the same time." Even our Lord Jesus Christ seemed to lose hope and faith. When he hung upon a cross and was mocked by his executors, he cried out, "My God, my God, why hast thou forsaken me?"

If you are one of those that finds faith and hope hard to come by at times, you need to know that you are in pretty good company. Many of the great fathers and mothers of the faith have had an equally difficult time and were not afraid to say so. You probably would be surprised to learn, if you did not already know, that the first few verses in the Bible were written at a time when the chosen people of God were having a hard time believing that God existed, and if he did exist, that he cared.

Walter Brueggemann, who is probably the finest Old Testament scholar living today and who teaches at Columbia Theological Seminary in Atlanta, says in his commentary on the book of Genesis that this first chapter of Genesis was most likely written in the sixth century BC and was addressed to the exiles in Babylon. The chosen people of God, who had been led out of Egypt by Moses and taken to the Promised Land, had now been defeated by the Babylonian empire. Their brightest and best had been carried off into captivity. They felt abandoned and forgotten. All of the empirical evidence seemed to agree that the Babylonians and their gods controlled the future. The Babylonians had, it appeared, defeated the dreams of the God of Israel. The problem facing the faithful of the sixth century was to find a ground for faith when their experience seemed to deny the rule of God. The message sent to them in Genesis I is that underneath and behind the experience of the present moment is the presence of the God of Israel, who spoke the first word and will also speak the last. "In the beginning God." Its affirmation is that this is God's world, and this God can be trusted even in the face of contemporary data—which may include sickness, poverty, unemployment, loneliness, and every other experience of human abandonment. It is important for us to know that these verses from the book of Genesis do not constitute a scientific description, but a theological affirmation.

As this was a message of hope and faith to a people long ago who were finding faith hard to come by—so too is it a message for us today. "In the beginning God created the heavens and the earth." In spite of the evidence to the contrary, in spite of any and all experiences of abandonment and what often appears to be random evil and violence, this is still God's world. "In the beginning God created the heavens and the earth, and the earth was a formless void and darkness covered the face of the deep." Is that what life feels like to you sometimes? A formless void with darkness over the face of the deep? Are there days when life seems devoid of meaning and purpose, days when the darkness seems to cover all the joys of life? Is some personal darkness undermining your faith and eroding your hope? What kind of void exists in your life today? "And a wind from God swept over the face of the waters." God is present in the darkness and in the chaos as a brooding and mysterious presence. And in the midst of the darkness God speaks: "'Let there be light,' and there was light." And God began to bring order out of chaos and light out of darkness. He saw the beginning of his creation, and he declared that it was good.

If I have learned anything at all in my thirty years of ministry, it is that what Reinhold Neibuhr said is true: "It is hard to be sane and to be Christian at the same time." A popular definition of sanity is to be in touch with reality and to accept reality. To be sane is to be realistic as the world defines reality. To be Christian, on the other hand, is to live not under the domination of the present evidence, but it is to live by faith. And faith, according to the scripture, is "the evidence of things hoped for and the assurance of things not seen." It is to dream the impossible dream and to fight the impossible fight even when all the evidence says that it is hopeless.

Jurgen Moltmann, author of *Theology of Hope*, says that the issue confronting us today is how to be men and women of faith in what often appears to be a godless and Godforsaken world. The sign of faithlessness today is not an aggressive denial of the existence of God. It is not overt hostility toward the church, or wickedness run wild. Rather, it is what often sits in our pews on Sunday. It is resignation to the way things are. It is inertia and melancholy. It is timidity, weariness and not wanting to be what God requires of us. Paul was right when he wrote that we wrestle not with flesh and blood, but with the powers of the darkness. Our mass media assures us that self-satisfaction and self-enhancement should be our primary concern. Our capitulation to this dark deception is seen in the vast numbers of people who anesthetize their spiritual sensibilities with consumption, with getting and spending, with parties and numbing out on alcohol and drugs, and who bury their heads in the sands of reality and have given up on God's dream for the world and for all of His creation. Many of us have become captives, not in Babylon, but in a land of broken dreams and broken promises. Like the people of God who sat down besides the waters of Babylon and wept when they remembered Jerusalem, we too need to be reminded of the God who in the beginning created the heavens and the earth and who will speak the final word in the end. We need to be reminded that this God has given us the gifts necessary to live as men and women of faith even when the darkness of this present age threatens to undermine our faith.

What are these gifts? What are the gifts of God for the people of God? They are many. I will mention a few of them because I, like you, need to hear and be reminded of them.

We have been given the gift of a new identity. "Once you were no people, but now you are God's people." Hardly a day goes by when I do not read about or hear about or talk to someone who is trying to find themselves. Plagued with the question of identity, they quit jobs, quit marriages, break promises, and break the hearts of others all in the name of some quest to find themselves. The Bible does not keep us in suspense about our identity. It gets right to it. We are children of God. We have been created in God's image to live in the world as his representatives. You can go into the far country of faithlessness and wander in a wilderness of confusion and despair about life and others; but if you live long enough, you will come to yourself and, like the prodigal of old, return to your father's house to be welcomed, not as a servant, but as sons and daughters of the father. Who are you? You are a child of God. You have been created and placed in the world to work, not for the exploitation and abuse of the world, but for the well-being of the world. Regardless of your status, your worldly success, the size of your bank account, or the number of accolades upon your walls, you are somebody! You are a child of God! You are a member of the household of faith and citizen of the kingdom of God—the only kingdom that has any real and lasting future! That is a gift that God has given you. You can live like you are nobody, but one of the gifts of God for the people of God is the gift of identity.

We have been given the gift of light. The spirit of God still broods over the darkness of our world and offers us direction and power. The God who created the heavens and the earth has given us his word, the Bible, to teach us what we are to believe concerning him and what duty he requires of us. Life is not a do-it-yourself affair. It is not something that we are required to make up as we go along. Long ago when God's people were in the wilderness, he gave them guidance. A pillar of cloud by day and fire by night, and he led them through. Is darkness threatening to overwhelm your life? Does the darkness of this present time make you feel lifeless? Do not despair. You are not alone. God has not abandoned us and left us as children with no parents. We have the light of his presence, for he has promised to be with us always—in good days and in bad—in joy and in sorrow. Even when we lose our hold on him, God will not lose his hold on us. The light shines in the darkness and the darkness has not and will not overcome it.

And God has given us the gift of hope. This hope is based not on what we have done. It is not based on our cunning, or our success, or even on our faithfulness. It is based instead on God. It is based on what God has done, on what God is doing, and on what God will do. When the painful and baffling circumstances of life become the seeds of despair in your life, remember what God has done. Remember that God brought a captive people home from Babylon. Remember that God led an enslaved people out of Egypt. Remember that God sent his only son to die for me and for you. In all the Good Friday moments of life remember Easter morning. Remember the hope that was given to John on the island of Patmos, where he was a prisoner with no earthly reason to hope. There he had a vision of a kingdom that was coming when there would be not more suffering or pain or death. God would speak the final word.

These are some of the gifts of God for the people of God. Receive these gifts. Treasure these gifts, and live your life with love, with hope, and with faith.

ONE MORE MOUNTAIN TO CLIMB

THE TRANSFIGURATION OF THE LORD
Matthew 17: 1-9

Are there places in your life that are sacred places? Is there some geographic spot or some memorable moment along the way of your pilgrimage where something wonderful happened?

All of us have places that are sacred. Your sacred place may be that place or moment where you first felt loved by the person with whom you have shared your life. It may be a place where you finally came to terms with what you were going to spend your life doing, or a place where you finally decided you were not going to do something you had been doing ever again.

Deep in the mountains of western North Carolina is one of my sacred places. You may have been there. It is not far from Montreat, along the Blue Ridge Parkway at a place called Craggy Gardens. Leaving the parking lot, you follow a path that leads like a tunnel through the laurel thickets, and then through a high meadow of blueberry bushes, until the path brings you to the top of the mountain where there is a large rock. Standing on the rock, you can look off to the west and down a long valley. The view is magnificent. On certain days in the early spring when the air still has the bite of winter, you can sit on that rock and watch the clouds and fog pile up on the southwestern face of the mountain. The wind blowing up the valley finally collides with the mountain, and there it piles up the fog and clouds. Then, like an inverted waterfall, it lifts them skyward—so close you can almost reach out and wet your hands in the dense clouds. To go there alone, to sit and experience all of that, leaves one feeling that in spite of all the horror that exists in our modern world, there is still a wonder and goodness about the world that defies description. It is a sacred place for me because at that spot I feel a sense of unity with the world. There in that quiet place I have, on occasions, felt a powerful sense of the presence of God.

That is finally what makes a sacred place sacred. It is a place or moment when the power and awesomeness of God is made manifest, and we experience his transforming presence.

Much of what we find in the Bible has to do with sacred moments and sacred places. The gospel lesson for today is a story of a sacred place. It also happened on a mountaintop. It is the story of the transfiguration of the Lord. The memory of this event is recorded in each of the synoptic gospels. For the first century Christian community, it was obviously an important memory.

In the midst of his travels, in between the grasping hands of the sick that were always reaching out to be healed and the hostile scribes and Pharisees trying to trap or discredit him, Jesus invites three of his close friends to go with him up on the mountain. It was not an unusual thing for Jesus to draw aside for prayer and quiet time. This time something else happened. The disciples saw their teacher transfigured before them. His garments became glistening white. Elijah and Moses appeared and were talking to Jesus. It was wonderful.

Peter could not contain himself. Finally something spiritual was taking place. They had been following Jesus around the countryside for months, and all that they had to show for it were some blistered feet, sleeping on the ground or at anyone's home who would provide them a bed, and a lot of strange paradoxical words about saving your life by losing it. They hadn't seen the first angel. Most of what they had been doing looked a lot more like social work than religious work. So it really was good to go up on the mountain and finally have something that felt like a spiritual experience.

That's a nice story, isn't it? It's what a lot of people want when they come to church: a spiritual high moment, up on the mountaintop, far from the problems and horrors of the world. *Don't talk about war in the church, or about the needs of the poor, the dispossessed, and the victims of oppression. Don't talk about politics or the need for personal involvement in the problems of the world. I come to church to hear about the things of God and to have some brief moment in the peaceful light of the transfigured Jesus.* I can relate to that. Can you?

Lifted out of context, this passage gives aid and comfort to all of that kind of thinking and wishing. But it is precisely the context of the story that gives us an insight into what Matthew wanted us to hear when he recorded this sacred moment.

In the preceding passage Matthew has recorded two of the more difficult sayings of Jesus: "If any man would come after me, let him deny himself and follow me. For whoever would save his life will lose it." Right after the event Jesus tells them not to talk about this until he is risen from the dead—and the disciples have no idea what he means by such talk.

This story of the transfiguration of the Lord seems strangely out of place and intrusive, but I believe that Matthew wanted the reader to notice the contrast. As it is in our time, so it must have been in the first century church. People were becoming a part of the Christian community with some hope that this would be an easy way to escape the world. Then, as now, there were those who came seeking a way of escape from the harsh encounters of ordinary living.

If you have come here today in search of a sacred place or moment that will help you separate from the world of pain and suffering, the world of war and injustice, the world of hurt and hopelessness, then look carefully at this sacred moment and remember the words that the disciples heard. "This is my beloved son; listen to him."

This lesson is about obedience. Up on the mountaintop, the disciples were given one more mountain to climb. Being a disciple does not mean that we are always in search of some mountaintop moment that separates us from the problems of ordinary living. Being a disciple means climbing the mountain of obedience. Obedience is at the very heart of discipleship. Obedient discipleship is the opposite of living in a random, self-seeking, self-serving fashion. It is the opposite of spending your money, your time, and your life on anything that gives you pleasure, the opposite of seeking to insulate yourself from the needs of the world. Disobedient disciples simply call Jesus when they need him and pay no attention to his teachings in the give and take of business, or in the decisions about how money and resources are to be used. In this memory of a sacred place, the disciples received an expanded understanding of their calling.

This incident gives us a clue to what a truly sacred moment and sacred place will look like. A sacred moment will always contain, even in a veiled way, an invitation to enter more fully into the kingdom of God. This sacred place can be an interior place or an exterior place. It can be any place and every place. Encounters with friends or strangers can be sacred moments. It can take place in a dream when something seems to challenge your former life and calls you to do something that you have never done before. At sacred moments and in sacred places where we meet God, we are always given one more mountain to climb: a mountain called obedience.

What mountain of obedience is God calling you to climb today? Is it a mountain of service to others that will break you out of a valley of selfishness? Is there someone you need to forgive? Someone you need to be reconciled with? Look at your own life. Are you kind to people, or is your life characterized by impatience?

An encounter with the God of all the worlds is always a mountaintop experience, but it always leaves us with one more mountain to climb. He calls us to live our lives in such a way that we will be instruments of his love and acceptance. He calls us to do things that matter.

One more mountain to climb. A mountain of obedience which leads to a mountain of personal transfiguration. When we are obedient to the God who calls us at some sacred place, we will discover that every place will become a sacred place, and in the journey we will be transfigured.

Lent: Repentance and Preparation

Lent is the forty-day period, excluding Sundays, before Easter. It begins on Ash Wednesday and ends on the Saturday before Easter. Sundays are excluded from the forty days of Lent because Sunday is the day of Christ's resurrection, making it an inappropriate day to fast and mourn for our sins. The season is called *Lent* because this is the Old English word for spring. Lent is forty days long because forty is a traditional number for discipline, devotion and preparation in the Bible. Moses stayed on the Mountain of God for forty days. The spies were in the land for forty days. Elijah traveled for forty days before he reached the cave where he had his vision. Nineveh was given forty days to repent. Our Lord spent forty days in the wilderness in preparation for the beginning of his public ministry. Lent is a time when Christians are called upon to imitate the forty days that Jesus spent in the wilderness. The time of Lent should be devoted to reflection, repentance, and preparation for the celebration of the resurrection of Jesus on Easter.

IS NEW LIFE POSSIBLE?

Genesis 17:1-10; 15-19 Romans 4: 16-25 Mark 8:31-38

What do you think of Abraham laughing in the face of God? In response to God's mighty promise that this old man and his aged wife would become parents, in response to this invitation to believe that new life is possible, Abraham falls on his face and laughs.

Paul speaks of Abraham as a man of faith. There is no ambiguity in the description of him that is offered in the fourth chapter of Romans by Paul. The apostle tells us that Abraham did not weaken in faith—that no distrust made him waver, and that he was fully convinced that God was able to do what he had promised. These words do not, however, match the description of the Abraham that God encounters in the seventeenth chapter of Genesis.

In this brief account, Abraham, the man of faith and the father of faith, is presented as the unfaithful one, unable to trust and quite willing and ready to rely on some other alternative. From a rational point of view, it is a totally appropriate response. Abraham has lived a long time. He is no optimistic enthusiast: in response to God's invitation to believe the promise, he demonstrates a scornful skepticism.

But who can blame him for his difficulty in believing? As we gather here today, we are invited to engage in an act that says we believe in the promises of God. We are invited to take the cup of salvation and call upon the name of the Lord. We are invited to believe, and to trust, and to ignore all the evidence of our life experiences and of reason.

In his great commentary on the book of Romans, Karl Barth puts his finger on the problem when he says, "Everything by which we are surrounded conflicts with true promises of God. He promises us immortality, but we are encompassed with mortality and corruption. He pronounces that we are righteous in his sight, but we are engulfed in sin." The weight of the evidence and the conclusions of reason say, *God's words are useless and impossible, stupid, petty and trivial, mendacious and preposterous.* The temptation that all of us confront in the call to faith is the temptation to scornful skepticism and disbelieving laughter.

Thus, in this moment of skeptical and scornful laughter there is something of every man and every woman in Abraham. In a world of random and chaotic events, in a world that seems to be filled more with demons than with anything else, can anyone believe that new life is possible? Can anyone really risk taking God at his word? Is not the call to faith a call to disregard the evidence? Certainly that must have been the way Abraham heard it, when told that God would make Abraham a parent when all the evidence of this world said "impossible." God's offer of new life was more than just the promise of a son; it was an invitation to covenant and to living a life, not in the light of the evidence, but in the light of the promise.

I have no difficulty understanding Abraham's scornful laughter. In the midst of the horrors that often confront us in this world, I find it painfully difficult to go on believing the promise.

64

Let us be honest with one another this morning. It is not easy to live in this tension, between the world as we experience it and the world God promises. There are times when I quite literally don't want to believe, because to believe places claims upon me that are painfully difficult in the face of the physical evidence. To believe requires that I view the world as potentially good and potentially loving, and there are days when that is hard to do. To believe requires that I affirm that somewhere, hidden in all the chaos and randomness of life, there are still signs of God's grace and a light that still shines in the darkness—and there are days when I see no signs of that grace and do not even wish to look for the light. To believe the promises requires that I affirm that forgiveness is better than revenge, and that love is better and ultimately more powerful than hate and force—and there are days for me, and I suspect for you, when I not only do not believe that, but do not want to believe that.

So there is no great struggle involved for me to understand the scornful laughter of Abraham. Life always presents us with the temptation to trust reason and experience, and to refuse to believe God. If I believe that, in spite of all the evidence, the promises are true, then much is required of me. In a world where circumstances seem to regularly crucify our faith, it is easier and more comfortable to agree with that cynical proverb, "He who expects nothing will not be disappointed."

Did it ever occur to you that somewhere in the heart of each disciple there might have been a feeling of relief when Jesus was crucified? Did not that awful event confirm what they really believed in their hearts? *The way it was before we met him was, in fact, the way it really is. Hate is stronger than love. Darkness is more powerful than light. Evil is everywhere. Life will crush you. No one can be trusted.* The dreamer was dead and with him the dream. Now they were set free from all the claims that the dream places upon them. The invitation to live a faithful and loving life in a dark and hostile world was no longer binding. Perhaps somewhere in the secret places of their hearts, they laughed a scornful laugh at themselves for ever having believed, and breathed a sigh of relief and went back to their fishing business. Can you understand? If it was not true, then there were no painful claims upon them. No crosses to bear. No gospel to proclaim. No need to love and forgive broken and hurting humanity.

William Meuhl tells a story that gets to the heart of the matter. In a community where there was no Sunday School except at the Unitarian Church, he decided to send his daughter there. One day she came home in a state of great excitement. "What happened at Sunday School?" he asked. His daughter quickly responded, "Susie said that Jesus was crucified and was dead and buried, but that on the third day he rose from the dead, and little Bobby Richards slapped her."

Could it not be that little Bobby Richards is in all of us? Maybe the resurrection is always bad news before it is good news. Because if we believe it, and if we give ourselves to the promise that new life is possible, then we must struggle to be obedient to the hope. If we allow the promise of God to lay more claim upon our lives than do the painful experiences of life, then we must offer our fainting, doubting hearts to God and pray for the gift of faith.

And it must also be said that in the final analysis, faith is a gift. It was that gift of faith that was finally given to Abraham. It is comforting to know that finally God's grace overcame the doubts of old Father Abraham.

Perhaps that is the best we can say about ourselves today. Left to our own reason and our own efforts, we would be swept away by the forces of darkness. We know that faith cannot be sustained by our grit and determination, but must be daily resurrected by the power and grace of God. There are days when we do not even want to believe, but we have come here again—perhaps laughing at ourselves for engaging in such an irrational act—but at the same time hoping and wondering if maybe again, today, God will give us the gift of faith.

SLOUCHING TOWARDS BETHLEHEM

Jeremiah 28:1-9 Psalm 84 Hebrews 12:18-29 Luke 13:22-30

There is something about the times in which we live that carries me back to my childhood. I don't remember if it was a single evening for several summers or several evenings in a single summer, but I do remember gathering with many neighborhood children at a house down at the corner and across the street. As the hot summer day cooled and the twilight settled in upon us, we gathered to play hide and seek.

"Someone has to be it!"

A child was chosen or volunteered. The person who was "it" would close his eyes and count to 100. The rest of us would hide. Off we ran to find a special hiding place where we would not be discovered. No one wanted to be moving or exposed when the seeker came to look. We found our hiding place and were as still as we could possibly be. Then the quiet of the evening was broken by the call of the boy or girl who was "it."

"Coming—ready or not!"

Do you remember some twilight August evening when you played hide and seek? I have never quite understood the appeal, but sometimes when I stand in the quiet of the summer twilight I find myself listening to see if I can still hear: "Coming—ready or not!"

I don't hear those words. I have not heard them for a long time, but when I read grim stories about wars and weapons, children and starvation, death and AIDS, unemployment and homelessness, broken families and broken dreams, I have the sense that something may be "coming, ready or not."

William Butler Yeats must have felt the same thing when he wrote a poem entitled "The Second Coming."
Turning and turning in the widening gyre
The falcon cannot hear the falconer;
Things fall apart; the center cannot hold;

67

Mere anarchy is loosed upon the world,
The blood-dimmed tide is loosed, and everywhere
The ceremony of innocence is drowned;
The best lack all conviction, while the worst
Are full of passionate intensity. . . .
And what rough beast, its hour come round at last,
Slouches toward Bethlehem to be born?

Things do seem to be coming to an end. Something new seems to be coming into being. As we move toward the end of the 20th century, the 21st century is "coming, ready or not." The world is radically different from the world of 1989 or 1990. The old maps are wrong. What is coming? What rough beast is slouching toward Bethlehem to be born? Is it really morning in America? Or do the spread of AIDS, the outbreak of civil wars, the spread of famine, the signs of environmental catastrophe, signal a twilight time and a darkness that is seeping in upon us? Something seems to be coming, ready or not. Is there any word from the Lord about how we should live in these changing, anxious times?

"He went on his way through towns and villages, teaching, and journeying toward Jerusalem. And some one said to him, "Lord, will those who are saved be few?" And he said to them, "Strive to enter by the narrow door; for many, I tell you, will seek to enter and will not be able. When once the householder has risen up and shut the door, you will begin to stand outside and to knock at the door, saying, 'Lord, open to us.' He will answer you, 'I do not know where you come from.' Then you will begin to say, 'We ate and drank in your presence, and you taught in our streets.' But he will say, 'I tell you I do not know where you come from; depart from me, all you workers of iniquity!' There you will weep and gnash your teeth, when you see Abraham and Isaac and Jacob and all the prophets in the kingdom of God and you yourselves thrust out. And men will come from north and south, and sit at table in the kingdom of God. And behold, some are last who will be first, and some are first who will be last."
(Luke 13:22-30)

Jesus is journeying toward Jerusalem. There is a sense of urgency. Time is running out. Something is about to happen. It is "coming, ready or not." This one who John called "Emmanuel, God with us" moves toward a confrontation with the powers and principalities of his age. His presence and his gospel would cause disturbance and resistance then, as it does now.

The gospel of Jesus Christ tells us that we are children of God in a world that tells us that we are here to do what we want and have what we want. The gospel of Jesus Christ tells us that the purpose of life is to represent God and his love, mercy, and justice; not to be anxious about food or clothes, house or wealth, but to be anxious about and work for the kingdom of God. That is a word that clashes with the powers and principalities of our time. The gospel of Jesus Christ calls you to pay attention to where God is at work in your life and to follow him into the Jerusalem places of our modern world. Jesus Christ calls us in this church, and in every church, to work for cities that are safe and just. As we have committed ourselves to care for the children in our midst, Jesus Christ calls us to be concerned about and work for the well-being of *all* of God's children. The ministry of Jesus Christ found its culmination in Jerusalem, but we must not forget Bethlehem.

Bethlehem is a symbol of hope, of new possibility, of something coming into being that will make all things new. But we live in a time when there seem to be many beasts slouching toward Bethlehem to destroy or undermine hope and newness.

The signs of the time call not for curiosity, but for repentance; not for idle curiosity about whom God loves, but for careful, prayerful reflection on how we should be living in the midst of this present age.

But those in the crowd then—like many in our world today—were wondering about the wrong thing. Rather than hearing and seeing the signs of the time as an occasion for urgent self-examination and repentance, the crowd seems to focus on abstract speculation about how many will be saved. Someone in the crowd asks, "Lord, will those who are saved be few?" They have not heard that what is limited is not the numbers, but the time.

And so it is with many of us. We engage in abstract speculation about who is good and who is bad, who is on God's side and who is not. We come to church and ask if God will be on our side—if God will help us be among the few that will be saved as we move anxiously toward the 21st century.

"Lord, will those who are saved be few?"

"Wrong question!" Jesus seems to say. The issue is not how many. The issue is you and your life. The issue that confronts us in our time is not salvation, but vocation. As converted men and women, what have we been set free to do, in the midst of all these things that seem to threaten so many in our time? As men and women who have been baptized, what are we charged and empowered to do?

Don't concern yourself with how many, but concern yourself with righteous living. Speculative abstraction is an evasion of personal responsibility.

"Strive to enter by the narrow door, for many, I tell you, will seek to enter and will not be able."

The word "strive" in the Greek is the root from which we derive the word "agony." Agonize to enter by the narrow door. It is not easy to be faithful in our time. It is not easy to be a faithful church. It is not easy to be a faithful minister or a faithful elder or deacon in the Presbyterian Church. It is no easy matter to know what God would have us to do, as individuals and as a church, but it is also no trivial matter. It is worth agonizing about.

There is something in the image that Jesus uses—the image of the narrow door—that makes me think of the birth process. God desires to be born in your life. In baptism we are impregnated with the presence of God, and it is our task to care for that fragile presence within each of us. Good prenatal care requires responsibility, diligence, good nutrition and the avoidance of those things that could harm the fetus. If a woman went to her obstetrician and said that what she is really concerned about is how few babies will be born healthy, I suspect that her doctor would tell her not to worry about that, but rather to concern herself with giving the best prenatal care she can to the baby that is growing inside of her. So it is with spiritual birthing. Good spiritual prenatal care requires responsibility, diligence, good spiritual nutrition and the avoidance of those things that could result in injury to that precious presence that God has placed in each of us. Could it be possible that many of our churches are little more than

70

spiritual abortion clinics, because we have not challenged persons to care for the precious presence of God within them?

Jesus says to you and to me: "You strive, you agonize, about the care you give to God's gift of his presence in your life. How everything else is going to turn out is not your question to answer; your question is about what you are going to do."

Your calling, and my calling, and the calling of this church, is to do what we can to make ourselves available to be used by God in the work that God is doing to heal a suffering world. Our calling as a church is to strive to be obedient and to offer ourselves as God's instruments as he is at work in Charleston and in the world. It is no trivial matter that is before us.

We live in a time when many things threaten our future and undermine our hope. The problems often seem overwhelming. The good news in this passage is that the world, or western civilization, or world peace, or the salvation of men and women, does not depend on you or on me. That is God's business. You must answer for you. I must answer for me. We in this church must answer for what we do, in this place and in this time. We are not saved because we strive and agonize about the kingdom. We strive and agonize because we are saved.

But where is the good news?

The good news is that God's grace is not limited to a few. Men and women will come from north and south and from east and west and sit at table in the kingdom of God. It will break down all geographical, nationalistic, and racial boundaries. Those that we think are last may well turn out to be first, and those that we assume are first may turn out to be last.

The good news is that there is still time. There is still time for us to repent and care for the gift of grace that has been given to each of us. There is still time to strive to enter the narrow door.

But there is a warning. The warning is that time can run out. You can wait too long and find the door closed.

Speculating about our own salvation is not what we are called to do. Speculating about who is an insider and who is an outsider is not what we are called to do. We are called to be God's people in God's world.

Now is the moment of decision. By God's grace there is still time.

Do You Believe In God?

II Chronicles 36:14-23 Ephesians 2:4-10 John 3:14-21

When I lived in the mountains of Western North Carolina, Spring always had a way of surprising me. Fall stripped the leaves from the trees. The deep cold of dark winter turned the grass brown and seemed to kill all but the heartiest plants and bushes. Deep in the winter, one could find no sign of life to suggest that spring would ever come again. The frigid days would come and go. There was nothing to suggest that anything would free us from winter's relentless grip. Then, in a surprising way, everything would begin to change.

Suddenly one day I would see, quite unexpectedly, a hint of yellow out beside the large elm tree in my front yard. Two days later it would be more than a hint. It would be a note of color amidst the winter quiet. A crocus was blooming. The first sign of life returning. In the days that followed, it was as if some unseen conductor were calling all the plants to joyfulness. Forsythia joined the symphony while Dogwood waited expectantly, poised to join in announcing the end of winter. Daffodils provided their own staccato as they splashed yellow here and there. Grass turned green again and trees broke forth in bud. Suddenly there was a crescendo of color. The whole earth seemed to be singing.

Every year it was a new surprise. Just when it begins to feel as if winter has spoken the final word—just when I begin to suspect that the season of cold and waiting is the season of reality—spring comes and surprises me with its brilliance, its life, its possibility!

But life is full of surprises.

We are taught—or we observe—or we are battered into believing—that this is true and that is not. We stake our lives upon some insight. We organize our days around some truth. An insight or truth that serves us well until suddenly one day something happens, and all that we have built our lives upon is challenged. Just when we think we have finally come to terms with how it really is, something happens that says, "Perhaps that's not the way it is at all."

I believe that is what happened to Nicodemus. John tells us that Nicodemus was a Pharisee. He was at the very top in the national cabinet called the Sanhedrin. The Pharisees were custodians of a great tradition and were viewed as experts in the field of theology. They believed that if they kept the law, salvation would be theirs. They, more than anyone in their culture, had God and life all figured out. They were careful, conscientious, law-abiding men. They were insiders in a system that left the foreigner, the broken, and the lawbreaker outside. Nicodemus was a Pharisee. Like all Pharisees, he really believed in the law. Obedience would give meaning to his life and secure him a place in the Kingdom of God. All the external evidence seemed to suggest that his way was right and true.

There is a sense in which Nicodemus represents all men and women who believe that they have life all figured out and that their way is best and right. Men and women who believe that they don't really need anyone but themselves. They can make it on their own.

The theologians call it salvation by works. We say we don't believe it. The way we live, however, is often at variance with our confession of faith. Not only do many of us believe in salvation by works, we also seem to enjoy that belief.

Believing that I can work it all out with no help from God or neighbor leaves me feeling pretty smug—until something happens that suggests that maybe the first will not be first at all. Maybe there is more to life than what I know. Maybe there is more to life than the right theology or the right degree. Maybe there really is no way to have it all figured out. Maybe there is no way to be sure that I can be "the master of my fate and the captain of my soul."

John tells us that Nicodemus came to Jesus in the night. We do not know why he came. We do not know what surprising thing happened that caused him to wonder about all the things he thought were true and all the things he had staked his life upon.

What could have happened to Nicodemus? Did he lose a child? Had he lost a sister through some meaningless act of violence? Had he watched an aged parent die a long and painful death? Was his marriage over? Had his business failed? Did the pain in the chest, that lingered and would not go away, suggest to him that time was running out? Or had he one day, for some unknown reason, taken his life and spread all of its bits and pieces before him and wondered what they meant?

Perhaps it was nothing more than a moment not unlike a moment described by W. H. Auden: "O plunge your hands in water,/ Plunge them in up to the wrist;/ Stare, stare in the basin /And wonder what you've missed." What had Nicodemus missed?

We do not know, but it surely seems that something was missing. If there was ever a person that many of us might identify with, it is Nicodemus: a careful, upright, law abiding man who wanted things done decently and in order. He came by night to consult with Jesus. He came in a clandestine way to ask this itinerant rabbi of questionable origin about the meaning of life.

And so it is with us. It is often in some kind of personal nighttime that we bring our lives, our values, and our most cherished beliefs to Jesus for reflection and conversation.

Lying awake in bed at three o'clock in the morning. . . pacing the floor with a concern that will not be still and will not go away. You've done it the right way. At least the best you knew how—and two plus two still turns out to be three.

What do you call such times in your life? Those nighttime moments when, in the darkness, you suddenly see some disturbing, surprising light. What you thought you knew with total clarity and assuredness—you do not know at all.

In the nighttime—in the dark time—in the questioning time—we slip away from the answers and solutions that we have constructed. Feeling a little foolish and very vulnerable, we come to Jesus.

We come because *our* solutions have become heavy and burdensome. We come because our answers don't work any more. They are too small for the big questions. They are suddenly inadequate for the horrors and the bad surprises. They no longer provide support when our lives suddenly feel like houses built upon the sand, and the floods of circumstance seems to be undermining every firm spot on which we have ever stood.

And in the darkness, and out of our darkness, we, like Nicodemus, come to Jesus and begin to discover the truth that will set us free.

Suddenly, for the first time in our lives, we begin to catch a glimpse of good news that is finally, really good. The notion that we really are in charge and that we can finally save ourselves through good works, or good scholarship, or good theology, or spirituality, or right living, or hard work, is not good news. It is bad news. To believe that peace, joy and wholeness is a personal, boot-strap operation is the worst news of all, because all the moments of surprising and disturbing light that have come to me have revealed, as much as anything else, my own neediness and frailty. In the nighttime moments of my life I have seen with awful clarity that none of my little systems will finally work. Left to my own devices, I am without hope.

So what is the point of it all? The point is that you cannot do it yourself. It is not as neat as we would like for it to be. We are not in control. Of all the dark deceptions that may capture us in this world, the darkest of all is the notion that I really am the master of my fate and the captain of my soul. To believe that notion is not to believe in Him, but it is to believe in myself.

Nicodemus and all his learned friends really believed in themselves and in their ability to do what was needed. He believed that—until something happened, and in the nighttime of his life he caught a glimpse of the light and things began to change. Nicodemus began to get free.

To Nicodemus Jesus said, God is not a system. God is not a set of rules that you can manipulate. The meaning of life is not a result of your own efforts; it is a gift of God. It is like the wind. It blows where it will. You do not know where it goes or where it comes from. You cannot control it. You can only trust it. You can only believe in the one who saved a people long ago, and trust that he will love us, who are no more lovable than they were.

"As Moses lifted up the serpent in the wilderness, so must the son of man be lifted up, that whoever believes in him may have eternal life." Our hope is not in ourselves. It is in the cross of Christ. Not because we are good, but because He is good.

Do you believe in him? Or do you believe in you? Do you believe in God or do you believe in America, in force, in race, or simply in your own ability to make it all have meaning? Nicodemus came to Jesus in the night because, at some level of his awareness, he had begun to doubt his ability to do it himself.

What happened to Nicodemus?

He assisted Joseph of Arimathaea with the body of the man who argued with him about his system and offered him freedom. One man has said that "Nicodemus became haunted by the distant sound of the wind. He began to suspect that there was more to the relationship between God and his creatures than merely a law." Nicodemus discovered in that nighttime encounter that "God is a lover who wishes to possess and to be possessed, and to be known not merely as information but to be experienced as friend, as Lord, as Savior."

"For by grace we have been saved by faith, and this is not our own doing – it is a gift of God."

THE QUINTESSENTIAL PILGRIM

PALM SUNDAY
Matthew 21:1-11

It had begun in the wilderness. It would end in the city. It had begun in a place where all definitions were set aside. There he had confronted his temptations. There he had wrestled with the implications of his call. It would end in the city, where men and councils created their own order and established their own definitions. The beginning was marked by a voice from heaven that said, "This is my beloved son in whom I am well pleased." The end would be announced by an angry crowd, shouting, "Give us Barabbas, crucify Jesus!"

And crucify him they did. With such a gruesome, painful and unjustified ending, one might suspect that the people of the city did not recognize him. But that is not true. They recognized him surely enough when he rode into their city. They called him, "Son of David, Prophet of Galilee." They waved palm branches, shouted "Hosanna" and called him blessed: "Blessed is he who comes in the name of the Lord."

And he did come in the name of the Lord. All the signs were there. He acted out the prophecy of old to be sure that his true identity would not be missed. The prophet Isaiah had listed the things that characterized the presence of God's anointed. The blind would receive sight, the lame walk, the deaf would hear, lepers would be cleansed and the dead would be raised. And don't forget the poor—the poor would have good news preached to them. From the very beginning these were the things that marked his ministry. So it was no surprise that they recognized him. What is surprising is how quickly and easily the shouts of "Hosanna" changed to cries of "Crucify him!" What is surprising is how something that started off so well ended up so badly.

Reading the Palm Sunday story is like seeing a movie that did not end the way you think it should have ended. I read recently about a person who, as a child, used to go back over and over again to see movies that ended badly. She believed that for these movies there was an alternative ending, a different final reel that the projectionist could show and make the story come out right. Perhaps we feel that way about the Palm Sunday story. But there is no other ending. Every year we come back to it and we read it again, but it still comes out the same way. He came into the city as a fulfillment of the prophecy of old. He did what the promised Messiah was supposed to have done. They welcomed him. They recognized him as one who came in the name of the Lord. He disturbed them and they rejected him. They arrested him, tried him, and crucified him. It will not come out differently. It is a perfect example of the shallow and fickle loyalties of people. It is not clear why their welcome changed so abruptly to shouts of "Crucify him!" It is not clear what the story really means.

It has always been easier to find meaning in the events of Maundy Thursday, Good Friday, and certainly much easier to find significance in Easter. For a long time it was hard for me to find much meaning in the Palm Sunday story. But what is really the point of Palm Sunday? Is it simply a fact that every year it is retold and rehearsed, full of sound and fury and palm branches, but not signifying very much? Or does it mean something? Are there lessons to be learned from it?

So often such stories in the Bible do not readily reveal their secrets. They stand before us mute, and we must sit in their presence and wait for them to reveal their lessons to us. When we sit before this moment in time, do we simply hear it as a particular and peculiar moment in history, or is it an event that happens again and again? Is there something archetypal about the story? I understand that Good Friday was an actual day—the day on which Jesus was crucified—but I also see Good Friday as a way of thinking about all the tragic, senseless, unjust experiences that come in life, that defy understanding, and make the love of God look like a mockery. In every life that endures for a while, there are Good Friday days, when all good hopes seem to die and there appears to be no justice. In the midst of our Good Fridays we wait, and hope and long for Easter. Is the same true of Palm Sunday? Are there Palm Sundays in every life?

I believe there are. I believe that we often have as much difficulty welcoming those moments in our life as did the crowds of long ago who first welcomed Jesus and then turned on him. What is

79

Palm Sunday? Palm Sunday is an intrusive moment. Jesus has quit preaching and gone to meddling. We tell ourselves that whatever the gospel means, it must mean that God wants to help us with our agenda. It must mean that God deals with us like an overindulgent and too-permissive parent who wants his child to get ahead and be happy. It must mean that God is at my service and Jesus has come to help me be more successful, more fulfilled, more whatever it is that I want. Palm Sunday began to go bad when it became clear that Jesus was a threat to the way things were organized in the city of Jerusalem. Jesus was most welcome when it was believed that he would help you with illness, raise Brother from the dead, cure Cousin's blindness, make the demons go away; but he does not stop there. He wants to redirect life. On Palm Sunday it becomes clear that when God enters our lives, he not only blesses, heals, teaches and leads; he also confronts and disturbs. Palm Sunday is the moment when it becomes clear that God is concerned with more than our spiritual and physical health. He is concerned with our moral health and has claims on the power centers of our lives. You see, we have little trouble with Jesus in the suburbs, or even with Jesus in the hospital. But Palm Sunday reminds us that God is not satisfied with being Lord of our spiritual lives or our inner lives—that is easy enough—but on Palm Sunday, Jesus goes downtown. He enters the law offices, the financial districts, the brokerage houses and the halls of government, and that is where the trouble really got started.

Palm Sunday happens when we discover and hear that God has not entered our lives to help us do our work, but that he has come to call us back to do his work. Palm Sunday happens when something takes place that disturbs the normal commerce of our daily lives. It happens when the spirit of God challenges the way our faith has entered into partnership with our pocketbook and our religion into the service of our national interest. Jesus was welcomed because it was expected that he would be of service to the city and of service to the national ambitions of the Jews, but instead he called the city to repentance. Whenever our lives are disturbed in that way, Palm Sunday happens, and until something has happened that challenges the way we think of life and of ourselves, we have probably not met the real Jesus.

It is always disturbing when God enters our lives. We can respond to that disturbance with hostility and rejection, or we can welcome him as liberator and life-giver, as one who comes in the name of the Lord. Over and over again in the Bible, the initial response of people to the intrusion of God is a response of fear. But over and over we hear God's gracious words: "Be not afraid." The only reason we need to fear when in the presence of God, is if we are more committed to keeping things the way they are than we are open to welcoming him into our lives.

The great question of the Palm Sunday event is the question that was asked long ago. Who is this? It is an unpleasant intrusion into an otherwise ordered life. Is it some neurotic manifestation? Should it be dealt with by drugs or psychotherapy? Or is it God who has gone and disturbed the normal commerce and definitions of our too-well-ordered lives? Some time ago, I spent one afternoon with an old friend in another city. He is a successful physician. But that which has always been so well ordered has suddenly begun to feel disordered. He told me that he had always been completely in control of everything that happened, but now he felt out of control. That which he had believed about life, about himself and his family, is no longer tenable. "Am I losing my mind?" he asked. Then he said, "Perhaps there is something else here, perhaps all of this has something to do with God in my life, or with the absence of God. Something is happening to me that I do not understand and that seems beyond my control." Could it be Palm Sunday?

"Be not afraid. It is I."

"Hosanna! Blessed is he who comes in the name of the Lord."

But that is not all that I see in this event. It is not just an example of what God's intrusion into the power centers of our lives will look like, but also an example of what our lives are supposed to look like. We see in Jesus the ultimate example of the fully human life. And that is what we have been called to be: a pilgrim people. Pilgrims are people who are passing through, citizens of another kingdom who travel from one holy place to another, unencumbered by lesser loyalties and ties. The pilgrim is called to travel light in the world, and so it was with Jesus. He amassed no fortune. He left no will. The poor man had nothing to leave. As the pilgrim moves deeper into the journey, his conception of what is essential changes. The trails of pilgrims are strewn with excess baggage. The further Jesus went, the lighter was his load.

The admonition that we find in Philippians is what it boils down to for us. "Have this mind among yourselves, which you have in Christ Jesus, who, though he was in the form of God, did not count equality with God a thing to be grasped, but emptied himself, taking the form of a servant, and became obedient unto death, even death on a cross." That is part of what Palm Sunday means. It is a demonstration of what our true humanity looks like: free enough from lesser loyalties to be God's representatives even in the midst of the city, to speak the name of God and to come in the name of God without embarrassment. Ours is not an agenda of accommodation. It is an agenda of transformation.

The whole reason for Lent has been to get somewhere. Like pilgrims telling the Canterbury tales, we have brought out our best stories. Up to today they have been happy-ending stories. Jesus in the wilderness is victorious over the power of Satan. At the well he changes a woman's life by his willingness to allow her to minister to him. A man born blind is made well and whole. And last Sunday's drama ended beside a tomb as Lazarus responds to the command of Jesus to come out. But today there is not a happy ending, and we are reminded that if we are to find our way through the dangerous and difficult events of Passion Week to the far side—to Easter and to new life—then we must be pilgrims. We must be liberated from lesser loyalties. We must be emptied of our pride, of our ambition, of our fears, and follow Jesus as he leads us deeper and deeper into the city.

BEYOND INTROSPECTION

John 13:31-35

What do you do when you don't know what to do? How do you get on with living when what has happened, or what is about to happen, is so catastrophic that the normal, ordinary responsibilities of life no longer seem important?

Have you ever had some crisis break into your life that made it seem impossible for you to think about anything else? Most of us have had such an experience. The death of a loved one, the failure of a marriage, a dream unfulfilled, loss of health, a hope broken, the premature departure of a child from home, and all events that have the power to undermine our ability to get on with the normal responsibilities of life.

Anyone who has ever lost a loved one knows how dominating that experience can be. In the days that follow the death of a significant other, the fact of that death is the first thing that is thought about in the morning and often the last thing thought about before sleep finally comes at the end of the day. Much time and energy is spent reflecting on how one should live in the meantime.

Crisis moments trigger introspection. They cause us to look inward, examine our actions, our values, and our decisions about the future. When a child leaves home, we may find ourselves thinking about what we should have done or should not have done. Standing before a disturbed or hurting marriage, we wonder about the future and often find hope hard to come by.

Several years ago a friend of mine was touring in Europe. Her travels finally took her to the memorial at Dachau. A part of that memorial is a small theater that shows a film depicting the events of that awful place. Recalling leaving that theater, she wrote:

Filing out of the theater in a line like any other tourist line, hunched and intermittently polite, are the tourists we have seen and been at every other place. They carry cameras, daypacks and shopping bags. They wear "I love Vienna" T-shirts and Heineken beer suspenders, baggy

Levi's and running shoes. Many of them look like nice people. What happened in this place is as remote from each of us as Pluto or the backside of our unconscious, as near to us as loneliness or hunger or thirst. My current preoccupations include the uncomfortable discovery that I no longer feel certain or even care about recent beliefs or decisions I had arrived at regarding my future life and work. A crisis of faith happens just when you think you've outgrown them.

In the face of catastrophic events, or the memory of such events, we pause and wonder about the meaning of life and about our place in it all. We look for something to believe in and something to which we can give our life and energy. At times all we can find is death, chaos, decay, broken promises, bodies that wear out too soon, and hopes that will be forever unrealized. "Change and decay in all around I see. . . ."

What does it all mean? What is it all for? What do I do now?

Such introspection can be useful if it leads to some insight and constructive amendment of one's life. Socrates said that "the unexamined life is not worth living," and that is probably true. Yet this introspection, which can lead to important insight and to significant change, can also become a prison that keeps us from getting on with the business of living.

While the Christian faith encourages introspection that leads to repentance, it is clear that the teaching of our Lord does not allow us to stop and settle for introspection as the goal of our journey. In those moments of his ministry when the words he spoke or the events that forced their way into his life triggered reflection and self-examination, Jesus quickly pointed his disciples to their responsibility to be involved in creative living in the world.

In the 13th chapter of John's gospel, we find our Lord's instructions to a group of men who were bogged down within themselves. We find words about what to do, given to men who did not know what to do. We find in this lesson a helpful word to all of us when we feel so overwhelmed by the circumstances of our lives that we feel unable to act.

Jesus has gathered his friends together in the Upper Room. His departure is imminent. Death leans against the door, demanding to be satisfied. Inside the room a conspirator aids death.

"One of you will betray me," Jesus says.

Something was about to happen that was catastrophic. In the face of this fact, the focus of the disciples' energy shifts. For a few moments their attention shifts to themselves. For a few moments their attention moves from his words to the memories of their own weakness.

"Who is it? Is it I? Am I the one who will fail when the testing time comes?"

Something in our lives begins to unravel. A call comes in the night that reports the dying of a brother. . . the pain in the chest grows worse. . . out of the blue your spouse tells you that the love that at one time filled the marriage is only a memory. . . and in those moments, like the disciples, we wonder about the meaning of it all—or the lack of meaning. The ordinary things seem no longer significant. What do you do in the midst of such life-changing, disturbing revelations?

Confronted with the news of his death, the death of their friend and teacher, confronted with the news of their own potential infidelity—"one of you will betray me" — the disciples wondered what it all meant. But Jesus moved quickly to call them to focus their energy not on the catastrophic nature of his death or on the disturbing revelation about their lack of dependability. Rather, he called them quickly out of and beyond their introspection, to focus their attention and energy on others.

"A new commandment I give unto you. Love one another, even as I have loved you."

Just when everything seemed to be falling apart, he spoke to them of responsibility. Just when they saw how frail and weak life is and how frail and weak was their own ability to live up to their promises, he called them to acts of greatness.

"Love one another, even as I have loved you."

In fact, he says, this will be the identifying mark of this fellowship. This is no abstract instruction that is given. No call to simply feel something. Rather, it is a commandment to do something. Love is something you do.

"Love one another," Jesus said, "even as I have loved you."

When health fails, when life leads us through some valley or disappointment, when we are confronted with the evidence of man's inhumanity which lives in the memorials of all the Dachaus of the world, when friends disappoint us and life leads us down roads we never planned to travel, the Lord calls us to love one another, even as he has loved us.

And that is precisely what he did—even to the end he loved his friends and his enemies. He prayed for those who were his persecutors and detractors. He asked forgiveness for his executioners.

It is to this kind of loving and this kind of living that he calls us. And this call is one that is given in the sunshine days of life as well as in the days when we wonder if anything matters or if there is any reason to go on.

He calls us to a love that becomes incarnate in action.

It is unfortunate but true that many in the church believe that love is simply something you feel. There is the notion that love is simply the warm feeling that one gets in church when something is said that moves you. Or when a child is baptized and we feel touched. Such moments may be the seeds of love, but it is not love until it gets beyond feeling and introspection to some kind of doing, living commitment. He calls us to love one another as he loved. That love was incarnational. It was love in action, in ministry, in lifestyle.

This is not an easy thing that we are called to do. It will mean we must struggle to love the stranger, the enemy, those who have hurt us or betrayed us. For it is precisely this kind of person that Jesus loved when he loved his disciples. It is precisely this kind of person that Jesus loves when he loves me and he loves you. He loves the person who does not deserve to be loved. He loves this person
86

who is often trapped in some prison of introspection. His love never gives up on us. It never quits. It continues to reveal itself in action.

What do you do when you don't know what to do? How do you get on with living when what has happened, or what is about to happen, is so catastrophic that the normal, ordinary responsibilities of life no longer seem important?

In such moments Jesus challenges us to move beyond introspection.He gives us a new commandment: "Love one another, even as I have loved you."

FAITHFUL LIVING IN A FAITHLESS WORLD

Acts 17:22-31   Psalm 66:8-20   1 Peter 3:13-22   John 14:15-21

How do you live, and what do you do when all the evidence you can muster seems to suggest that life is a rat race and the rats are winning? How do you live, and what do you do when the scorekeepers of the world make it appear that the wicked prosper, the guilty go unpunished and the powers of darkness seem to be pushing back all the signs of light? What do you do, and how do you live, when everything that you have loved and staked your life on seems to be falling apart and there seems to be no one or no thing that you can trust or depend on?

These are not easy questions to answer in the abstract, and certainly not easy to answer when they are questions that emerge out of our life experiences. But these are important questions for all of us. They are especially important for all who claim to be men and women of faith. Jurgen Moltmann, author of *Theology of Hope*, has written that the critical issue for Christians living in the 20th century is how to be men and women of faith in what often appears to be a godless and Godforsaken world.

These are the questions that I invite you to consider with me this morning. Let us look again at the gospel lesson from John and see if we can find some answers. I believe that John 14:15-21 offers us a clue to what faithful living looks like in the midst of a world that appears unconcerned about faith at best, and godless and God-forsaken at worst.

John 14:15-21 is a small portion of the conversation Jesus had with his disciples in the upper room as they shared their last supper together. They had gathered to celebrate the Passover and remember the mighty act of God when He delivered the children of Israel out of Egypt. They were remembering a God who brought hope and direction to a people who were hopeless and enslaved. It was there in the midst of that Passover meal that Jesus began to speak of what lay before him. He spoke of his death that would happen the next day. He told them that he would be leaving them. He told them that one of their number would betray him. These are some of Jesus' last words at the last supper. In order to fully appreciate what he is saying, it is important for us to try to imagine what the disciples must have been thinking and feeling.

Here we have a group of men who have left everything behind to follow Jesus. They have staked their lives on his message and on his teaching. They have been tired together. They have been cold and hungry together. They have experienced rejection and suspicion together. Through it all they have believed that he was the Messiah and the kingdom that he announced was on the verge of coming into being. Now the whole thing seems to be coming unraveled. The crowds that cheered him into Jerusalem have turned hostile. The authorities are moving to arrest him. Jesus is going to be tried and put to death. Only God knows what will happen to them now. The worst news of all is that one of the trusted twelve is a traitor. Can you imagine what they were feeling there in that upper room? This room was not filled with the joy of victory, but was permeated by the agony of defeat and failure.

Can you make a connection with those men in that room? Can you take the bits and pieces of your life and hold them in your hand before you, and find some moment in your past or present that feels like that moment? Was it a moment when a friend betrayed you? Was it a moment when all the things that you had tried to do seemed to be for nothing? Was it a moment when a relationship broke apart and you knew it would never be fixed? I imagine that every one of us has had some "Last Supper" experience: a moment in time when you came face to face with the hard reality of injustice; a moment when you experienced the hurt of failure and the sharp, stabbing pain of betrayal. I believe that the disciples were feeling all of those feelings. What have you felt like doing when those moments broke over you and into your life? Did you simply want to quit the field because the battle seemed to be lost? Were you tempted to join the forces of evil and darkness and strike back in anger, because if you can't beat them you might as well join them?

The disciples heard the bad news about the future. They loved their teacher. They did not want him to leave them. What were they to do?

Listen to these brief words of wisdom and direction from our Lord: "If you love me, keep my commandments."

There in a nutshell is what faithful living looks like. Don't sit around and get bogged down in self-pity, or make lists of your enemies, or rage against the unfairness of life. Instead, Jesus said, do your duty. Do what I have taught you to do. When everything is going well, when God seems to be in his heaven and all seems to be right with the world, it is not hard to have hope and live in a positive way. But our Lord gave these words to men living through a moment when their world was tumbling in about them. Everything seemed to suggest that the forces of evil would win the day. All the evidence seemed to agree that the forces of darkness were stronger than the forces of light. "Never mind," Jesus said. "Pay no attention to the evidence. Draw no conclusion from the way things look today. I have chosen you. I love you. You love me. Keep my commandments."

These words are not unlike the words of Jeremiah to the exiles in Babylon. For the exiles there seemed to be no hope. All had been lost. The exiles, carried off into captivity in a foreign land, sent word back home to Jeremiah. "What are we to do? How long before we will be delivered?" And the word came back. "Deliverance will come; but not in your lifetime. In the meantime, build houses and live in them. Plant gardens and eat their produce. Work for the welfare of the city where you find yourself, for in its welfare will be your welfare." When you are living in the meantime of hopelessness, do the things that your hands find to do.

"If you love me," Jesus said, "keep my commandments."

Part of the problem that we have with this direction is that it is so foreign to what the world is teaching us today. The age in which we live might well be called an "Age of Victimization." There is hardly a group in our society that does not blame someone else for its problems. The poor blame the rich. The Democrats blame the Republicans. The blacks blame the whites. Gays blame straights and straights blame gays. Women blame men. Children blame parents. And we all blame our dysfunctional families. But this is not really new. It is as old as Adam who said, when God confronted him with his disobedience, "This women that you gave me, she disobeyed and she tempted me. It is really your fault, God."

This is a far cry from a tombstone I saw which said simply, "HE DID HIS DUTY."

On the second floor of the Confederate Home there is a memorial to one of the founders. This home was created in a dark time. Charleston was poor. The future was bleak. But a woman named Isabel Snowden did not blame the North, or the world, or God. She did not sit down and feel sorry for herself, or give in to her feelings. She joined with others to create a home and a safe haven for poor women. Her memorial reads: "Founder, Isabel Snowden, February 20, 1881. A Martha to the homeless poor, a Mary in her love." She loved Jesus, and in the hard times, she kept his commandments.

What does faithful and successful living look like?

Faithful living is more concerned with duty than with rights. Faithful living seeks to make things better rather than seeking to find someone to blame.

Faithful living is more concerned with the well-being of the neighbor than with one's own well-being. Faithful living is God-centered living and not self-centered living.

Faithful living is guided by the word of God rather than by the wisdom of this world. Faithful living is grace-filled living rather than judgment-filled living. Faithful living is grounded on the promises of God and not on the promises of this present evil age.

How do you live, and what do you do, when it appears that the wicked prosper and the guilty go unpunished? Jesus said it very clearly: "Keep my commandments." Do your duty. Live a life that is run by your commitments and your promises, rather than a life that is controlled by whatever you may be feeling at any given moment.

"But," you say, "that is too hard. It is not in me to do it." Jesus knew it would be hard, and so he promised us the presence of the Holy Spirit. He promised us his presence: "I will not leave you desolate," or like children without a parent. "I will come to you."

The direction to be obedient is followed with a promise. You are not alone. God will come and be with you and in you and give you the strength to do what you have been called to do, but you must begin by admitting that, left to your own devices, you will fail.

When we surrender the direction and control of our lives to Jesus, then he gives us the power to do what we have been called to do.

One final word. We know something that the world does not know. We know something the world does not believe. I like the way this was stated by an elderly Baptist preacher from Philadelphia: "It's Friday, but Sunday's coming." In the fourteenth chapter of John's gospel, it is Maundy Thursday, but Sunday is coming. It will soon be Good Friday, but Sunday is coming. It looks like darkness and betrayal and evil will speak the final word, but Sunday—Easter Sunday—is coming. We know that on Easter the disciples got a glimpse of the future. They learned the secret—that Death will not speak the final word. Failure will not speak the final word. Sickness or betrayal or broken homes or broken hearts will not speak the final word. God will speak the final word.

Do you love Jesus? Do you want to live a life of faithfulness? Do you want your life to be successful and make a difference in God's eternal story? Then keep his commandments. Is that too hard? He will send his Spirit and he will help us. Is life too discouraging or overwhelming? Maybe so. But remember, when moments of hopelessness threaten to undermine your ability to hope:

It's Friday, but Sunday is coming!

Easter: New Life and New Hope

For Christians, Easter is the day on which the resurrection of Jesus is celebrated, but it does not find its origins in the Christian community. These second-century Christian missionaries traveled among the Teutonic tribes north of Rome. Whenever possible, they transformed pagan customs to harmonize with Christian doctrine. On a practical basis, this prevented local converts from being persecuted by pagan traditionalists. The pagan festival of Eastra, which celebrated the coming of spring, coincided with the Christian observance of the resurrection of Christ. Eastra was represented by a rabbit (read: Easter Bunny), and eggs have been symbols of new life back to the time of the Egyptians.

In the Christian Church, Eastertide or the Easter season begins on Easter Sunday and continues until Pentecost, and spans a total of seven weeks. It is the most important season in the Christian Year.

In the Christian community Easter recalls the fact that Jesus was brought from death to life, and reminds Christians that with God, nothing is finally hopeless. In John's vision in the book of Revelation, God speaks to him and says, "Behold, I make all things new." During this season especially, believers are invited to live with hope.

THE RESURRECTION: A METAPHOR OF HOPE

EASTER SUNDAY

Isaiah 25:6-9   I Corinthians 15:1-11   John 20:1-18

One dark and moonless night, a tramp, looking for a dry and quiet place to sleep, slipped into a cemetery. Suddenly he stumbled over a pile of dirt and fell into an open grave. For nearly an hour he struggled to climb out of the newly-dug grave, but the sides were smooth and his efforts were fruitless. Weary with his efforts, he sat down in the corner of the grave to wait until daylight and the possibility of help.

A little later, another man cut through the same cemetery. He was coming home from a party where the alcohol had freely flowed, and he walked with an unsteady step. He encountered the same mound of dirt and fell into the open grave. But he did not notice that the grave contained the tired tramp. The tipsy stranger tried over and over to climb out of the grave. When he began to attempt to high-jump out of the grave, the tramp finally broke the silence, saying, "You can't get out of here!" But he did.

According to William Bausch in a book entitled *Storytelling*, it is an ancient Russian Orthodox tradition to celebrate Easter by telling jokes even in church. Bausch says, "They felt that they were imitating that cosmic joke that God pulled on Satan in the resurrection." The powers of darkness seemed to have spoken the last word. Jesus is in the grave and Satan says, "You can't get out of here"—but he did.

It may not seem like a joke to you, but on Easter Sunday the church announces with word and song that there is good news from the cemetery. He is not dead! He is risen! To the age-old question, "If a man dies, will he live again?" Easter responds with an overpowering "YES!" Will death speak the final word? God's answer in the Easter event is "NO!"—only God will speak the final word. Easter is God's YES to death's NO!

But that is not all that Easter is!

94

If you hear the Easter message as simply an answer to your questions about life after death, then you have failed to grasp the most powerful part of the Easter message.

The real power of the Easter message is contained in the fact that Easter is not just God's answer to our question about death; it is also God's question to us about life.

The way in which each one of us answers the Easter question will determine the way in which our lives are empowered and liberated by this good news from the cemetery.

Writing to the church at Corinth, Paul speaks about the resurrection. He lists the various individuals and groups to whom the risen Christ has appeared. And then he says something that moves me every time I read it. "And finally," Paul says, "he appeared to me."

"He appeared to me!"

For Paul this is the pivotal moment in his life. This was the moment that had made all of the difference—this personal encounter with the risen Christ. Paul believed in the resurrection. But more than believing in it as an historical reality with future implications, Paul had experienced the power of the resurrection, and its life-changing force.

God's question for us is this: Do you believe in the resurrection as a present possibility for your life?

Do you believe that the power of the risen Christ can be a power in your relationships? Do you look for the appearance of the risen Christ in your living?

A man came to his pastor distressed about a marriage that had grown lifeless. They talked for a little while about the marriage, and how he felt about it. Finally the man put his finger on the nub of the problem. "I love my wife, Pastor, but I am not in love with her or she with me. Do you think that we can ever be in love again?"

The pastor paused and then asked this distressed man. "Do you believe in the resurrection?" The man looked at his pastor in disappointed amazement. "I'm talking about my marriage. I did not come to talk about theology or the Bible. Why did you ask me such a question?"

"Because," said the pastor, "if you believe in the resurrection, you will believe that there is hope even for a relationship that seems dead."

I have called this sermon "The Resurrection: A Metaphor of Hope." This is no suggestion that the resurrection was not an historical reality. I affirm that completely. What I am suggesting is that we use the historical resurrection event as a metaphor through which we look at the commonplace, ordinary events of our own lives.

A metaphor is like a filter. We look *through* it at the ordinary. It serves to bring into focus certain things that might otherwise be missed. To speak of the resurrection as a metaphor is to invite all of us to look through the resurrection at the ordinary events of our lives, with the anticipation that resurrection moments will be taking place there from time to time.

To believe in the resurrection means that we can never declare that any system is closed. We can never say that anything is really finally and ultimately hopeless. To say that anything is beyond hope is to say that it is beyond the power of God to make it new and different.

All of use metaphors to view and organize the experiences of our lives. The metaphors we choose tend to heighten certain events and to filter out others. If we believe that life is a "rat race," then that metaphor will heighten our sense of the frustrating, meaningless moments in our lives. If death and failure are our primary metaphors then it will be easy for us to miss the moments when the risen Christ appears to us in some place or moment when all that seemed to be over is renewed.

Do you see the power in this?

To believe in the resurrection means that we live not with despair, but with hope. It does not mean that we should stay in destructive marriages or continue forever in jobs that squeeze the life out of us, but it does mean that in every situation and in every place there is the possibility of something new and good taking place.

The question that God confronts us with on Easter is this: "Do I believe in the resurrection as a present possibility in my life—and do I look for the Easter moments in the routine moments of my living?"

Paul said that Jesus finally appeared to him. That turned his life around. That moment was more pivotal, more life-changing, more memorable, than any other moment in his life. When has Easter happened in your life?

Years ago I was leading a small group of people who were trying to recover from the pain of divorce and separation. We talked awhile about what it meant to be lonely. Finally one of them turned to me and said, "You listen to us talk about our loneliness. Are you ever lonely?"

At that moment in my life I was lonely, but did not think that there was anyone with whom I could share that fact. But with that surprising invitation I took the plunge and talked about my own feelings of loneliness.

In a place where I thought I was the helper, I became the helped, and Easter happened for me. In a strange place and in a strange moment the risen Christ appeared to me through the care of a wounded friend. Where two or three had gathered together in his name, there he was in their midst. Easter happened. Church happened!

Church happens wherever and whenever Easter happens. There can be no church if there has been no Easter. Paul wrote to the Corinthians and shared the memory of his personal Easter.

When has Easter happened in your life lately? What has happened to you lately that is really worth celebrating, worth giving a party to commemorate, worth laughing and singing about? Who have you shared your Easter moments with? Who have you told that the risen Christ has appeared to you in the kindness of a friend, in the caring of a stranger, or in the beauty of a springtime night? It is in the sharing of our Easter moments that the gospel is most authentically proclaimed.

We are here today because of the resurrection. The abandoned tomb into which we peer is not only the Lord's but our own. By the power of his resurrection we have been raised to new and lasting life. There are no closed systems. There is no situation that is beyond hope.

No Greater Love

John 15:9-17

A number of years ago I read about an experiment that was conducted in a home for babies abandoned by their parents. The babies were divided into two groups. One group was fed, clothed, washed and kept warm, but never held. The other group received exactly the same thing, but one thing more was given. These babies were held and caressed and received regular and continuing love. Before long it was clear that the babies in the first group were not developing properly, while the babies that received the loving care of their nurses were growing and developing well. The conclusion was no great surprise. In order to grow and develop, human beings need to be loved. In fact, there are those who believe that if a child receives no love, no visible signs of affection, then it is likely that the child will not survive. Each one of us here today is here because someone has loved us, and the person that loved us first was more than likely our mother. We may not have been loved enough. We may not have been loved as freely or as well as we might wish, but if you are here today, it is because someone has loved you.

The loss of love is probably the most painful experience that any human being can have. Several years ago I was conducting a workshop on grief and an older man in the group spoke of the death of his mother. "It is hard to lose someone that you love, but it harder to lose someone who loves you."

Jesus knew of the importance of love. In fact, he made it the identifying mark of his fellowship. In the upper room with his disciples on the night when he was arrested, he spoke to them of love. "This is my commandment, that you love one another, even as I have loved you. Greater love has no man than this: that he lay down his life for his friends." Not only did Jesus commend love to his disciples and he commends it to us, but he also offered through his life a clear picture of what genuine love looks like. Last week we looked at what Jesus had to say about the importance of being connected to him and the necessity of bearing fruit. Today I invite you to think with me for a little while about what is to characterize our lives if we are to be Christians who bear fruit. Jesus did not say to build great cities. He did not say to get rich and be successful in business. He did not say to be happy and to acquire many things. Rather, he said that we are to love one another.

What is this love that Jesus speaks of? Scott Peck, in his book *The Road Less Traveled*, says, "Love is too large, too deep ever to be understood or measured or limited within the framework of words." I agree, but I do believe that the Bible offers us some clues or guidelines to use in thinking about the love that Christ commands us to have for one another. This morning I want to offer you one thing that love is not, and four things that we *can* say about love, based on the scriptures.

First, love is not just a feeling. It is not just emotion or a sentiment or some kind of personal high. It is not just "romance." This feeling or emotion is what many of us mean when we talk about being "in love." Years ago a couple came to me and told of the estrangement that they felt in their marriage. I asked what they wanted to do, and they said, "We want to be in love with each other again." Nothing wrong with that, but if the relationship between two people is predicated on being "in love," then that relationship will not last. Yesterday I conducted a wedding here in the sanctuary, and I asked the couple to promise to love one another "until death do them part." I did not say, "as long as you are in love." I did not say, "as long as you have a warm feeling for one another." I said, "as long as you shall live." Now, I don't want to get into the whole area of divorce, but I do believe that many folk could work out their problems if they took that vow seriously. And this leads me to the first thing I want to say about what love is.

Love is more than a feeling. It may begin with a feeling, but it is a commitment. It is something we decide in our heads to do, and something we commit ourselves to do in sickness and in health, for richer or for poorer, in good days and in bad. It is a commitment to which others can hold us accountable. My wife taught me something important about love a number of years ago when I asked her why she had stayed married to me all of these years. We married very young. Statistically, we probably should not have been able to stay married. People who marry at eighteen and twenty-one often don't stay married today. I was hoping she would say that she stayed married to me because of some wonderful characteristic that I possessed, but she simply said, "Because I said I would." That is commitment. That is love. That is solid ground on which to stand.

Second, love is an act. Love is what mothers do when they get up at night and feed or hold a crying child. Love is what fathers do when they attend a school activity even when they don't think they have time, or when they get up every day and go to a job even when they don't enjoy going to that job, because they want to take care of their family. Love sits by the bed of a sick child in the hospital. Love cooks dinner and washes clothes and makes beds and wipes runny noses. Love calls or visits an aging parent. Love takes a lonely friend to lunch. Love listens to someone who pours out the pain of a broken heart. Love is not easy words or glib sentiments. It is something that you do.

Third, love is self-denial. The powers and principalities of this age whisper in our ear and tell us to satisfy ourselves first. To get all that you can for you, because you only go around once. But that is the voice of a liar and a thief. Love considers the fortunes of the beloved one to be as important to the lover as his own. Love does not exploit others. It does not say that I will love you if you meet my expectations, or if you are good to me, or if you do what I want, or if you meet my needs. Love says that what you want and what you need are as important as what I want and what I need. Love does not measure the quality of a relationship by the degree to which our needs are meet. Love denies self in order to be self-giving.

Fourth, love never quits. It is not a dependent commitment. It does not say, "I will love if you will love." Love is a unilateral commitment, and it never gives up no matter what the beloved does or does not do. The love that Christ has for us never quits. Christ did not say, "I will love you as long as you are faithful, or as long as you are dependable, or as long as you are interesting." Paul understood love that did not quit when he wrote in his Epistle to the Romans that "nothing can separate us from the love of God." Nothing! Do you hear that good news? Nothing in all creation can separate us from God's love, because that love never quits! Your depression, your anger, your smallness, your moral failures, your poor performance as a parent or a spouse, nothing in all creation can separate you from the love of God. That is how we are called to love. This is the love that

Jesus was speaking of when the lawyer came to him and asked what he must do to be saved. The lawyer asked using a verb that implied a single act. Jesus told him the story of the Good Samaritan and told him to go and do likewise, and to keep on doing that. Not one act of love, but a love that continued. Most of us are here today and are what we are because there was someone who refused to give up on us even when we were ready to give up on ourselves. Love never quits!

Fifth, love is forgiving. Love does not keep score. Love does not make and keep inventories of past failures. Love forgives, and love forgets. The scripture tells us that when God forgives us, our sins are removed from the book of God's remembrance and remembered against us no more. That's what the Bible means when it says that when we stand before God, we will stand clothed in the righteousness of Christ. Not clothed in sins long remembered, because when God forgives, God forgets, and our sins are remembered no more. Isn't that wonderful? Isn't it great when someone says they forgive us, and we never hear about it again! Any relationship that you have with another human being is going to have in it a degree of hurt and disappointment. All relationships are between two people who are sinners, and every now and then we will demonstrate our sinfulness to one another. And if we cannot forgive each other, we cannot love each other. A couple came to me once who were deeply estranged. They asked me if they should forgive one another. I said, of course you should forgive. For Christians forgiveness is not an option, it is a responsibility. Love is forgiving.

Finally, love is a gift. The Bible tells us that we love because God first loved us. It is a gift freely given. Lorraine Hansberry has a delightful play about a black family in Chicago: *A Raisin in the Sun*. The father dies and leaves about $10,000.00 to the family. The mother says that this will allow her to fulfill her dream to have her own home. The son of the household begs for the money. This young man has never had a chance, has never had a good job, but he has a friend who has invited him to go into business. He begs and finally the mother gives in and gives him the money, and you can guess what happens. The friend runs away with the money. The son comes home beaten and broken. The sister turns on him and tears him up. Then the mother turns to the sister and says: "I thought I taught you to love him." The sister says, "Love him? There is nothing left to love." Mama says, "There is always something left to love, and if you ain't learned that then you ain't learned nothing. Have you cried for that boy today? I don't mean for yourself and for your family because we lost the money. I mean for him because of what he has been through and for what it has done to him. Child, child, when do you think it's the time to love someone the most? When they have done good and made things easy for everyone? Then you ain't through learning, cause that ain't the time at all. It's when he's at his lowest, and he can't believe in himself cause the world's done whipped him so. When you start measuring someone, child, measure him right. Be sure you know what hills and valleys he's been through to get to where he is."

I don't know what you call that, but the Bible calls that grace. When you don't deserve love, and you get love. When you don't deserve to be cared for, and you are cared for. God loves you— not when you have done good, but in spite of what you have done or failed to do. The scripture says that "Where sin did abound, grace did more abound." Look around you. Is there someone that needs the gift of love?

How do we do this? Left to our own devices we can't do it. I can't do it. You can't do it. It's not in us to do what Jesus tells us to do. That's the bad news. But there is good news because the bad news is not the end of the story. Not only does Jesus call us to this greater love, but he promises us the power we need to do what he calls us to do. We can love because he first loved us. We can love because he stills loves us.

Do you want to love this way? How? Open the door of your life to Jesus Christ. He stands at the door and knocks. He will come in and give you a new heart and a new spirit. Quit trying to control your life and turn it over to Jesus. Put your life under new management. Open yourself to the God who promises that he can "do more abundantly than you can ask or think." And when you do this, you will begin to experience love, not as the world loves, but as the Lord loves. That is the greatest love of all, and you will finally understand what the Apostle Paul meant when he said, "I can do all things in him who strengthens me."

"Greater love has no man than this, that he lay down his life for his friends." That is what Jesus did for us, and that is what we are called to do for others. That is the good news of the gospel.

103

Pentecost

Pentecost was originally an Old Testament festival, calculated since the time of Josephus as beginning on the fiftieth day after the beginning of Passover. In the Christian calendar it falls on the seventh Sunday after Easter. In the Old Testament it was originally an agricultural festival celebrating and giving thanks for the first fruits of the early spring harvest. In the early New Testament period, it gradually lost its association with agriculture and became associated with the celebration of God's creation of His people and their religious history. The word "Pentecost" means fiftieth day, and the sanctuary color for Pentecost Sunday is red, the color of the church. The focus of the season is on the church's mission to the world, and the enabling presence of God through the work of the Holy Spirit. It is a time to call people to renewal through the work of the Holy Spirit in their lives.

YOUR PENTECOST MOMENT

Ezekiel 37:1-14   Acts 2:1-21   John 15:26-27, 16:4b-15

And now he was finally gone. He had been crucified, dead and buried. They thought then that it was over. They thought that he was gone forever. But three days later the word had come from the cemetery: "He is not here; he is risen."

And then for forty days he had appeared randomly, here and there among them—in a room, in a garden, on a road to Emmaeus, by the sea of Tiberius, on the beach. He spoke with them. He taught them. He touched them, and they touched him. He ate with them. He challenged them—but now he was gone.

He had been lifted from their sight into the clouds. Before his ascension he told them to stay in Jerusalem—the place where all the trouble had happened, the place where he was finally rejected, arrested, and crucified.

"Stay in Jerusalem," he said, "and wait for the gift of the Holy Spirit."

That is how the day of Pentecost begins for this little gathering. These who are now leaderless are waiting in Jerusalem.

It is Pentecost: an agricultural festival, but also a festival that recalls the gift of the law to Moses on Mount Sinai. In obedience to Jewish requirements, people have come from north and south and east and west to be present for this important event.

But in one house, perhaps in a single room, people wait. Not sure what they are waiting for, or even sure what they are to do in the meantime, they wait in obedience to their ascended teacher.

This is no remarkable gathering. Not one is famous, powerful, or wealthy. Many are demonstrated cowards. Many have proven that they are not finally dependable. Frequently they have been slow to understand. On occasion they have shown the unattractive signs of petty, self-centered behavior. A most ordinary gathering—and in fact, they are not unlike most of us gathered in this room today.

No Roman official in Jerusalem would have suspected them of being any kind of threat to the powers of Rome. The very idea would have been ludicrous. These folk were seen as no more of a threat to the powers of Rome than we would be seen as a threat to the powers and principalities of our time.

Not even sure what they were waiting for, they waited. They were living in the meantime. Something important had ended, and only God knew if there was something else that would happen.

Then it happened. There in that waiting place there was a sound like a rushing wind that filled the whole house. Something like fire seemed to descend upon each one of them. They were filled with the Holy Spirit. The spirit that had brooded over the waters and had brought order out of chaos now filled these ordinary folk. The spirit that breathed life into the bones in Ezekiel's valley now breathed new life into people whose hope was fast becoming as dry and dusty as dry bones.

To these waiting, a new sense of direction was provided. With that new sense of direction came the gifts and the energy to do the work that was now their work to do. On that Pentecost day when people had come from north and south and east and west to celebrate the first fruits of the harvest, a group of less than remarkable persons became the agents of God's first fruits. The church was born on Pentecost, and these less than spectacular people suddenly began to do spectacular things.

This day of Pentecost is an important memory in the life of the church. It is the memory of a moment of grace that was given to undeserving folk who were faithfully waiting.

Pentecost is an important memory to all of us in the church, but it is particularly important to men and women who are waiting: living in some kind of meantime between the end of something and a beginning that has not yet been revealed.

Perhaps many of us in this room are living in some kind of meantime. Waiting for grief to pass and wondering where we will find the vision and the energy to live in the future. Waiting for bodies to heal and wondering if real healing will ever come. Waiting for marriages to get better or for marriages to be over with. Waiting for children to finally work out their problems and to live normal, productive lives again. Waiting for a rebirth of hope and energy that will make each new day exciting.

Are you waiting today in some kind of personal Jerusalem where the powers and principalities—or perhaps the forces of randomness—have crucified your hope and crushed your dreams? Do you feel like you have been asked to sing the Lord's song in a foreign land and you wonder if that song is worth singing?

Pentecost is an important memory for the church, but it is particularly important for all of us who are waiting. It is an important memory for a great host of men and women who are living in some personal meantime.

Pentecost calls the church to remember that there is nothing that is beyond hope. No matter how hopeless the situation may seem, Pentecost invites us to wait with hope.

The gift of new hope, new direction, and new energy may not come with the sound of rushing wind or tongues of fire. God's spirit may be given to us on a most ordinary day while we are doing a most ordinary thing.

As Frederick Buechner reminds us in *The Sacred Journey*, "The question is not whether the things that happen to you are chance things or God's things because, of course, they are both at once. There is no chance thing through which God cannot speak - even the walk from the garage to the house that you have walked ten thousand times before, even the moments when you cannot believe there is a God who speaks at all anywhere. He speaks, I believe, and the words he speaks are incarnate in the flesh and blood of ourselves and of our own footsore and sacred journeys."

For all who are living in the meantime—waiting for new hope, new energy, new joy—remember Pentecost and look for your Pentecost moment. Remember Pentecost of long ago, and allow that memory to nurture your own anticipation of a moment in your time, when God will give you the gift of new direction, new energy, and a new vision for tomorrow.

Where will it happen? When will it happen? Only God knows, but this special memory that we hold before us today invites us to wait, not as men and women who have no hope, but to wait with eager anticipation. We wait for a time and a place where the Spirit will come like the wind and burn like the fire and will make all things new again.

Ordinary Time

The Second Vatican Council invented Ordinary Time, and the new liturgical calendar including it began on the first Sunday in Advent in 1969. Since then many Protestant Churches have also adopted the concept, which has won wide acceptance throughout the Christian community as a whole. The liturgical color for Ordinary Time is green, which symbolizes growth and hope. Ordinary Time does not mean common. "Ordinary" (ordinal or numbered) expresses order or succession. Ordinary Time reflects the rhythm and tempo of our lives. The season reflects on the mighty works of God through Jesus Christ. It is a time to grow in our faith in response to God's invitation to follow Jesus. We have a challenge to make our ordinary days extraordinary.

STANDING ON HOLY GROUND

Exodus 3:1-15

Have you ever felt that you have missed the meaning or possibility of your life because of some foolish choice that you have made, or because of something that has happened to you, or because the opportunities you hoped would come to you have not? A number of years ago I was talking with a woman who, if I recall correctly, was about 45 years old. Her children were in the midst of adolescence with all of the problems that often occur at that time. Her marriage was in disarray. Her profession no longer challenged her. As we talked she said a sad but interesting thing. She said, "This was not the way I planned or expected for things to be at this point in my life. Very little has turned out the way I expected. Now it seems too late to do anything about it."

The poet W. H. Auden may have been going through something similar when he wrote in one of his poems: "Stare, stare in the mirror, and wonder what you've missed." Do you ever wonder if you may have missed the point of your life? Are you here today feeling that you are trapped in a place that has no future or in a life that has no meaning? If any of these things are true, then the lesson from the

Old Testament that I read moments ago should be a word of good news for you. It is good news because it tells us about a God who does not abandon his people. It tells about a God who cares about lost men and women. It tells about a God who calls folk out of obscurity and hopelessness, and commissions them to go and be instrumental in bringing people out of slavery and into freedom. It recalls an event that happened long ago about a man who was interrupted by God in a wilderness place, and was given the opportunity to move out of obscurity and hopelessness and to become God's instrument in a mighty way. This story invites all of us who may be living through some wilderness moment to pay attention to what is happening, because we may find ourselves standing on holy ground. In fact, this story suggest to me that wilderness ground may have more potential for being holy ground than any other place. Let's think about that for a little while this morning and see if we hear a word of good news for us as individuals, a word of good news and challenge for us as a church, and a word of hope for the world.

This story of Moses and the burning bush is an important memory in the story of the people of God. I invite you today to recall this story with me and listen to hear in it a clue about how God works to redeem our lives from insignificance. It is also important because it shows us how God often works to bring people out of slavery and into freedom. While there is no other story in the Bible that is just like this story, the story is similar to many other stories in the Bible that tell of how God comes to people and calls them to a journey of faith.

We meet Moses in the second chapter of the book of Exodus. He was born in Egypt in a time when the Pharaoh had decreed that every male Hebrew child that was born should be cast into the Nile. Moses' mother manages to hide him for the first three months of his life, and then she placed him in the river in a basket. Moses' sister is left to watch and see what happens to little brother. The Pharaoh's daughter comes down to the river to bathe and notices the basket with the baby in it. She takes pity on the child and arranges for the child to be raised by a Hebrew woman (who was also Moses' real mother). When Moses gets a little older he is adopted by the Pharaoh's daughter and raised in the Pharaoh's house. Moses has every reason to think he had a bright future. But Moses makes a foolish choice. He sees an Egyptian guard beating a Hebrew. He attacks the Egyptian and kills him and hides his body in the sand. The next day a Hebrew says something to Moses that reveals to him that what he has done to the Egyptian is public knowledge. When the Pharaoh hears about it, he seeks to kill Moses. Moses flees for his life. He goes to Midian, east of Egypt, and eventually is connected up with Jethro, the priest of Midian. Jethro gives him one of his seven daughters for a wife, and Moses settles down to work for his father-in-law. This incident that I read from Exodus 3 takes place deep in the wilderness while Moses is tending the sheep. Notice that it doesn't happen while Moses is doing something religious, or as a result of some prayer by Moses. It happens unexpectedly while Moses is at work. The angel of the Lord appears to Moses in a flame of fire out of the midst of a bush—"the bush was burning, but it was not consumed." The fire did not go out. Moses turns aside to see this thing, and it is then that God calls him by name. God then tells Moses to take off his shoes, "for the place on which you are standing is holy ground."

Two things I want to call to your attention. The first is that Moses probably believed that he was pretty well stuck in Midian. He was a fugitive. Pharaoh wanted to kill him. We can imagine Moses sitting out there in the wilderness wondering what his life might have been like if he had not been so rash and foolish as to kill the Egyptian. Obviously his life is not turning out the way he expected. Moses is really a has-been, and he has no real future that has any significance. Then something happens. This is the second thing I want you to notice. There in that wilderness place he sees a fire that does not go out and a bush that is not consumed. He is confronted with something that cannot be explained and will not go away. And the scriptures tell us that God is present in this event, and this wilderness spot becomes holy ground.

How do we make a connection with this?

The first thing that seems important to pay attention to is the suggestion in this story that just when you think things are not working out the way you had planned, or your life has been interrupted by the results of some foolish choice, or by some event beyond your control—it is precisely in the midst of those moments that you may be most likely to be interrupted by God. We should look for God in the midst of those days and in those moments when life seems to be suddenly out of our control. The God that we meet and get to know in the Bible is a God who comes to us when our lives are in disarray or when we are least expecting him. He came to Jacob in a dream when Jacob was fleeing for his life from the anger of his brother. He came to Abraham in Ur of the Chaldees and called this man with a barren wife and no hope of progeny to be the father of a great nation. He revealed himself to Isaiah in the temple in a time of political turmoil and distress and said, "Whom shall we send, and who will go for us?" And Isaiah responded in faith and said, "Here am I Lord, send me."

This God that we meet in the Bible is a God who shows up in unexpected ways and unexpected times.

And finally in the fullness of time, we are told that the Word became flesh and dwelt among us. God came among us as a child born at Bethlehem—a child born to peasant parents who had no prospects for a meaningful future or a significant life, but who became the parents of one who was called "Emmanuel—God with us."

This story suggest that if you are here today and are living your way through some wilderness moment in your life—a broken home, a broken dream, a broken heart, a broken body, anything that has taken your hopes and dreams and dashed them upon the rocks of circumstance—don't be surprised if somewhere off on the periphery of your life experience, you see or feel something that is like a fire that will not go out and will not go away. It may wake you in the night and leave you sleepless in the morning. It may be a nagging anxiety that you feel as you live your way through painful days and troubled nights. Is God in those moments in a special way? I do not know, but this memory of a burning bush long ago suggests that we might do well to wonder if, in the midst of such moments, we may be standing on holy ground.

Holy ground for you may be a quiet and lonely moment in your kitchen when the children have gone to school and the chores are done and you struggle with something inside you that is like a fire that will not go out. It may be a quiet walk on the beach in the gathering darkness, when you take the bits and pieces of your life in your hands and wonder if what you are doing is what you should be doing, and you wonder if there is any possibility that you might do something that matters with your life, and it is like a fire that will not go out. Or holy ground may be a hospital room that you have been taken to because of cancer or a heart attack or something else that you did not expect, and you wonder if your days of usefulness are over, and in that quiet, wilderness place it is as if you hear someone calling your name—calling you to a new way of living and to a new kind of usefulness—and it is like a fire that will not go out.

I expect that all of us have stood on holy ground at one time or another and have been confronted by something that disturbed our sleep and troubled our days like a fire that would not go out. Perhaps we noticed and heard the word of the Lord in our ear—perhaps we did not. Perhaps we were too busy to hear the word of the Lord. So caught up in our schedule, so infatuated with our profession, so anesthetized by being so busy trying to live a life that mattered, that we did not hear the voice of God in our ear calling us to do something that, perhaps for the first time in our life, really did matter. How many times have we been like the people T. S. Eliot wrote about in his poem, "Ash Wednesday"? He wrote, "Where will the word be heard? Not here, there is not enough silence." Could it be that it is only in the wilderness moments that God is able to get our attention?

But what is it that God calls us to in these wilderness moments when we are standing on holy ground? Certainly there are times when we are called to do very specific things, in just the way that Moses was called to go up to Egypt and say to Pharaoh, "Let my people go!' But more times than not, it is a call simply to go on a journey, in the very way that Abraham was called to go on a journey. And in order to go on that journey of faith and faithfulness, it is necessary to leave some things behind and put our hand in the hand of God and allow him to lead us—even when we do not know where we are going. Perhaps he is calling us to detach ourselves from greed or ambition or seeking after pleasure. He called Abraham to leave family and tribe and home and go to a place that God would show him. Perhaps he is calling you today, in your wilderness moment, to let go of despair, or disappointment, or anger, or some need to get even, and to come and live in the light of a whole new set of values today. Perhaps he is speaking to you in your wilderness moment and calling you to represent, not your own interest, but to represent God's interest.

In order for Moses to answer the call that came to him, it was necessary that he leave his home in the wilderness. It was necessary to leave his business and his fear of Pharaoh. What is God calling you to let go of, in order to be his faithful man or woman? For Moses to answer the call, it was necessary for him to change his priorities and be obedient to the vision, and that was not an easy thing for him to do. He was able to come up with a lot of reasons why he could not do this, but God said to him—as he says to us—"I will give you what you need in order to do what I have called you to do, if you are faithful and if you trust me." Do you hear that? Whatever it is that God is calling you to do, he will supply you with what you need to do it.

There are lots of folk all around us who are living in some personal Egypt. Many of these folk are folk that God has put his mark on in baptism, but they are living in bondage to some kind of Pharaoh. You may be one of them. This God who came to Moses long ago is a God who cares—not only about lost people, but also about people in bondage to things that have no future. As a church, as a congregation, as individuals, I believe God wants us to be his instruments to bring about freedom and release to his people who are living in some personal Egypt. He wants us to go to them and tell them that God loves them and that Jesus died for them. He wants us to be his hands, to stand at the door of their places of bondage and knock upon the door in the name of Christ, to tell them about this one who came to seek and to save the lost.

If you are here today living your way through some wilderness place, then hear this. It doesn't really matter what you have done or failed to do. Jesus Christ died on a cross for you. He took your sins in his body. You have been washed in his blood. God has saved you so that you can be his representative and so that you can do his work. He wants you to be his man or his woman. He wants this church to be faithful, and he promises to give us what we will need to do the work that he calls us to do.

We are standing on holy ground, and to ignore the call of God that is coming to us in this wilderness time would be to miss the whole point of our lives. God forbid, Lord, that this should happen to us.

WORDS FROM THE WORD ABOUT WORSHIP

Isaiah 6:1-8   Psalm 28   Romans 12:1-8   John 4:1-26

Did you hear about the woman who hired a new maid, but was not satisfied with the work that she was doing? "Marie," she said, "I can write my name in the dust on this table." "Isn't that great?" Marie responded. "I can't write my name anywhere. It just goes to show what an education will do for you."

Marie had missed the point. It is my impression that many folk often miss the point when it comes to understanding what our corporate worship is all about. This morning I want you to think with me about what worship is supposed to be and to do, and I want us to do this in the light of the passages from Isaiah and John.

Whenever one begins to talk about worship and how it should be done, one runs the risk of getting into the kind of conversation that Jesus encountered when he met the Samaritan woman at the well. The incident that John describes is rather enigmatic. After some mysterious and tantalizing dialogue about water and living water, Jesus tells the Samaritan woman at the well to go and fetch her husband. The woman quickly replies, "I don't have one!" Jesus responds: "Woman, you're right to say you have no husband. You've already had five husbands, and the man you've got now is not your husband." Now at this point, the woman apparently feels that the conversation is about to get out of hand, and she makes an attempt to change the subject. Sensing that the man before her is some kind of religious teacher, she makes an effort to engage him in a theological discussion. "Sir, I do perceive that you are a prophet. Our fathers worshiped on this mountain; and you say that in Jerusalem is the place where men ought to worship."

Up until this point the conversation had been sufficiently symbolic for the woman to stay with it and remain comfortable, but suddenly the stranger quit preaching and began to meddle. At that point the woman did what we often do in church when someone says something that strikes too close to home. She changed the subject and tried to get Jesus into a conversation about theory and theology.

Jesus refuses to take the bait, but tells her simply, "The hour is coming and now is when true worshipers will worship in spirit and in truth."

Do you hear what he is saying? He does not respond to the question of where one should worship or when or what form should be used. Rather, Jesus says that true worship is worship that is done in spirit and in truth.

Thus, if we are going to talk about worship, it is more important to apply the criteria that Jesus used with the woman at the well than it is to wonder if it is Reformed, or Lutheran, or Baptist, or Catholic. Rather than get all bogged down in whether the offering should be here or there, or if the hymns should have five verses or three, or should be sung from the red hymnbook or the blue hymnbook, the real question that we should ask about our worship is this: Are we worshiping in spirit and in truth? What needs to be present for one to be engaged in true worship?

First, let us recognize that true worship is not something that can only happen on a particular day at a particular time in a particular place. True worship takes place when we have an encounter with the living God and when, in that encounter, we are led to a more accurate understanding of who God is, who we are, and what duty God requires of us. True worship can take place at any time or any place. One does not have to be much of a student of the Bible to know that the most significant encounters that the Bible records between God and his people did not take place in formal services of worship. God did not encounter Jacob in a worship service or a time of private devotions. Rather, he came to him as a stranger beside the river in the night and wrestled with him until the breaking of the day, and Jacob received a new name and a new identity. God did not call Moses at 11:00 AM on Sunday, but came to him in the heat of a workday and spoke to him from a burning bush, and Moses received a new understanding of the purpose of his life and a new direction for his future. God called the boy Samuel in the night while Samuel was serving in the household of Eli. Angels appeared to shepherds on a hillside while they were tending their sheep and told them of the birth of a savior. The Apostle Paul met his risen Lord in a vision on the road to Damascus, and in the scripture read today, a Samaritan woman meets God in the person of Jesus Christ in the middle of the day beside a well.

The moments in the Biblical record when folk perceive the reality and presence of God are far more on the side of ordinary moments than on the side of structured moments in some service of worship. But as my friend and former teacher, Dr. Shirley Guthrie, told me once, "God can work even in the church." And there are moments in the Bible when folk have true and profound experiences of true worship in planned and structured services. Perhaps the closest thing we can find to a significant encounter between God and man in a structured worship service is recorded in the 6th chapter of Isaiah. This event took place in the temple and provides us with a progressive account of the ingredients of this encounter. According to Isaiah, it took place in a time of national crisis and difficulty. It took place in the year that King Uzziah died. This suggests to me that we are more likely to experience the presence of God in times of difficulty and crisis than in times of peace and harmony.

We may be able to hear and see the working of the Lord when we have been shaken to the very core of our being by some disturbing life event. Perhaps it is the loss of health, or our marriage is threatened, or we are on the verge of losing our job, or our spouse dies, or a child breaks our heart. Isaiah came to church in the year that king Uzziah died. Perhaps you have come here today when something else either has died or is dying in your life. But it was at that time that Isaiah came to worship and experienced the presence of God in a mighty way.

His experience begins with a vision of the holiness and goodness of God. And Isaiah's response to that vision is an overwhelming sense of his own sinfulness and inadequacy. Isaiah confesses this: "Woe is me, for I am a man of unclean lips and I dwell in the midst of a people of unclean lips." But God does not leave Isaiah to wallow in his guilt, or to use it as an excuse for not drawing close, or to sink into some abyss of discouragement and self-accusation. A seraphim comes to him and touches his lips with a burning coal and says, "Behold, this has touched your lips. Your guilt is taken away and your sin is forgiven." Isaiah saw the holiness of God. Isaiah was cleansed of his guilt, but this was not all. Isaiah heard the word of the Lord and heard the call of the Lord and offered himself in response to that word. "Whom shall we send, and who will go for us?" And Isaiah does not hesitate or debate with himself, but responds immediately and clearly, "Here am I Lord, send me."

This is one of the clearest examples we can find in the Bible of true worship. It begins with God and concludes with Isaiah's response to God. It was a disturbing, life-changing event that took place not at Isaiah's initiative, but at God's initiative. It did not support Isaiah's previous self-esteem or view of himself, nor did he find in worship the encouragement to go on doing whatever he had been doing. To the contrary, Isaiah was given a new sense of his own acceptability to God, the gift of a new direction for his life, and the energy to pursue that new direction.

True worship takes place anytime we experience the overwhelming and life-changing presence of God. It is not something that we can control or that we can manipulate. The order of our service is not the critical event in our worship. John Harris in his book *Stress, Power, and Ministry* says that worship should loosen our hold on the illusion that we are in control of life. It is meant to break through our normal ways of looking at ourselves in the world. It is meant to move or shock us into an awareness of our vulnerability. By its very nature worship involves anxiety. While we can go through the forms, say the prayers, listen to the lessons read and the sermon preached, sing the hymns and repeat the creed, unless we have a sense of being in the presence of the living God, and in the presence of one in whom we live and move and have our being, then it is unlikely that what we have done could be called worship.

I believe that many of us, perhaps all of us at times, come to worship services in ways that fulfill John Wesley's definition of atheists. According to Wesley, atheists are not those who overtly deny God so much as those who, though they may be religious in a civic or churchly fashion, live as if God did not matter. Soren Kierkegaard described his fellow Christians in 19th-century Denmark as shop-keeping souls. They did their dull religious duty in order to satisfy a God whom they conceived not as a purifying flame of love, but as a dull balancer of debits and credits. Any worship experience that leaves me comfortable, is never disturbing or offensive in some way, is probably not true worship. Any service that leaves us comfortable and allows our perception of ourselves to go unchallenged, and either implicitly or explicitly supports my definitions about what is important and how my life should be lived, and leaves me not with anxiety, but with a warm drowsy glow, is a service that has invited us into the presence of some god *other* than the God who created the heavens and the earth, and the God who brought the Israelites out of Egypt with mighty power and wonders, and the God who broke open the tomb on Easter morning. True worship should leave us with a sense of wonder and awe. True worship will often cause us to confess, as the Psalmist did so long ago, "It is an awful thing to fall into the hands of the living God."

Do you come to worship expecting to hear the word of the Lord for you? Do you come to worship believing that your prayers will be answered and your life will be changed and healed? Or perhaps you come with no expectations at all. If God did speak to you or if God did answer your prayers, what would you do then? Perhaps it is better not to take this whole thing seriously, so we can go on living the way we do. Could it be that God is really dead for many of us because we dread for him to be alive?

In Walker Percy's novel *Love in the Ruins,* Percy tells of the experience of a man named Dr. Thomas Moore who describes himself as a bad Catholic. In the novel, Moore remembers why he did not take his daughter Samantha to Lourdes when she was dying of neuroblastoma. "I was afraid she might be cured," Moore confesses. "Suppose you ask God for a miracle and God says yes. How then do you live the rest of your life?" If we truly encountered the living God, or if he answered our prayers for our loved ones or our families or for us—if God cured our illness and rescued us from the darkness of our own paltry lives—how then would we live the rest of our lives? Isn't it easier never to ask so we will never know, and then be able to go through life holding on to our cynicism and our apathy—holding on to our illusions that we are the masters of our fate and the captains of our souls? Are we like the one described in Psalm 52 who "did not take God for a refuge, but who trusted in great wealth and relied upon wickedness?" Or are we like the writer of Psalm 28 who said, "The Lord is my strength and my shield; my heart trusts in you, and I have been helped?" Do we come to worship and slip into a drowsy stupor? And if by chance we do hear the word of the Lord, our response is, "Here am I, but for God's sake don't send me."

What is true worship? It is clear from even the few Biblical examples that I have referred to this morning that worship is not something that is limited to Sunday morning, but is an experience that can take place whenever we come into an encounter with the living God. What we do on Sunday morning may be a rehearsal, a practice, if you will, of what we expect to take place in those moments in life when God in his grace chooses to make himself known to us.

The fact that we use symbols, colors, music, sacraments, all serve to remind us that God may speak to us in a variety of ways. The fact that we worship together is a reminder that the most significant symbol of all is found in other people—people created in the image of God. It is often through other people that God will make himself known to us, if we have eyes to see and ears to hear. And true worship should sharpen our vision and improve our hearing. This service of worship provides us with an important clue to how our lives should be lived every day. Our days should begin with praise and end with service. Our days should be spent listening and watching to hear and see the word of the Lord that says to us "Whom shall I send and who will go for us?". Worship that is done in spirit and in truth will prepare us to say, "Here am I, Lord. Send me."

YOU HAVE BEEN BAPTIZED!

Exodus 14:19-31   Psalm 103   Romans 14:1-12   Matthew 18:21-35

Some of you know of my enjoyment of country music and of my appreciation for country music singer Willie Nelson in particular. In Willie's most recent album, *The Most Unoriginal Sin*, there is a song about two people trying to get over a relationship that failed. The singer says that this grief and hurt is almost more than they can deal with: "It's not as though my life ain't hard enough to do."

Life is hard to do sometimes.

Is your life hard to do?

Mine is at times. I suspect that's true for most of us. One of the things that makes life hard to do in this present time is the large number of conflicting and confusing voices that come to us in a variety of ways from our culture. There are narcissistic voices that tell us that the most important person to be concerned about is yourself. There are the voices of advertising that tell us that the purpose of life is to be a consumer and to get more and more things. There are the therapeutic voices that tell us that we should not be concerned with other people's problems, and that the goal of life is to find oneself and to be self-actualized—whatever that means. There was a time in our past when there seemed to be something of a consensus in our culture about what was right and what was wrong, but that is no longer true. The voices encourage us to do our own thing, but it is not clear what that is. That makes life hard to do.

But this confusion exists even in our churches. Old Testament Scholar Walter Brueggemann has said that in the church we are always in danger of something he calls "spiritual amnesia." We gather together, we do the things we do at church, but we are not sure, or do not quite remember, what they mean, or how they fit together, or what they have to do with the life we live from Monday through Saturday in this world of conflicting voices—and that makes life hard to do.

It is not just conflicting voices and confusing experiences in the church that make life hard to do. When we gather the bits and pieces of life together and sift through them, we find memories of hopes that were not realized, dreams that never came true, promises that were not kept, words of affirmation or forgiveness that were never spoken—and that makes life hard to do.

There are relationships that have not worked out; children we do not understand and who refuse to bless us with the gift of appreciation; acquaintances we thought were friends, but who, when things get heavy, turn and walk away—and that makes life hard to do.

We get sick with something for which there is no cure, or we get old and energies slip away and faculties erode, or we watch parents succumb to the ravages of aging, and someone we have known all our lives doesn't know who we are—and that makes life hard to do.

And then on the second Sunday in September in the year 1993, we come to church, hoping at some level that we will hear an encouraging word, a word of blessing, a word of hope or forgiveness or recognition, some word that will lighten the load and help to make the living of our days a little less hard to do.

I am sure that life was hard to do in the first century. Probably a lot harder to do than anything we have ever known. Perhaps it was some desire to make it a little easier that led folk to try to figure out such things as how many times to forgive someone who has hurt you, or wronged you, or betrayed you. Is once enough? Or should you do it three times, or maybe even seven? Matthew recalls that Peter came up to Jesus and said, "How often shall my brother sin against me, and I forgive him? As many as seven times?"

When can I give up on my family, or my siblings, or my parents, or my children, or my fellow church members? How many times do I have to say "I'm sorry" to a spouse who never says they are sorry? Give us a rule—a hard number that we can follow and know when we have done enough. That would make life a little easier to do. But Jesus doesn't do that. Instead he said, "I do not say to you seven times, but seventy times seven." Which was Jesus' way of saying that there is no limit to the number of times that you should forgive. And that sounds like it makes life *harder* to do—but then Jesus told a story.

Jesus was always telling stories to let us know something about God and his kingdom. The story is about a king who had a servant who was so deeply in debt that there was no way that he could ever pay. At first there seemed to be no hope. The servant begged for mercy, and the king forgave him all that he owed. More than seven times seventy. And this is the good news: the kingdom of heaven is like this. In the kingdom we can be liberated from past failures and mistakes and given new hope and possibility. And the rest of the story reminds us that in the kingdom, we have a responsibility to forgive others in the same extravagant, incredibly generous way. I don't have to decide if you deserve to be forgiven. I don't have to weigh the evidence to see if my child or my spouse or my friend deserves forgiveness. Rather, I forgive because that is the way that God has forgiven and will forgive me. God has blessed me and said, "You are forgiven." In the kingdom of heaven we will be blessed like that.

We all want a blessing, don't we? That would make life easier to do: if we knew that someone knew us through and through and loved us still and all. It would make life easier to do if we could hear a word of unconditional love and acceptance. It would make life easier to do if we could hear today, in this place, that we belong somewhere.

Walker Percy, in his book *The Gramercy Winner*, tells of a man in a tuberculosis sanitarium who is visited day after day by another patient. One day as the friend is leaving, the man calls after him, "Stay with me a little while longer. I'm homesick." "How long have you been homesick?" the man asks. "All my life," is the reply.

Does not that speak for all of us? There is in us a pervasive homesickness. St. Augustine spoke of it another way when he said, "Our hearts are restless until they rest in Thee, O Lord."

The stories in the Bible are about God coming to a slave people in Egypt who had no real home, to lead them out to a land that God would give them. Jesus said, "I go and prepare a place for you"—a home for you. "In my father's house are many mansions." In church I hear about my true home and my true family, and that makes life easier to do.

How do you know that you one of those rooms is for you? How do you know that you are a member of the family of faith and a citizen of the Kingdom of God?

Years ago, on a Sunday afternoon, on a day when my life seemed hard to do, I was visiting a friend at his place in the country by the river. Standing out in front of the house I saw a little band of folk gathering by the river. It was a small group from a local church. They had come for a baptizing. I drew closer and listened to the preacher as he stood in the river with two young girls and an old couple he was about to baptize. "I ain't worthy to do what I am about to do," he said, "but the Lord has called me to do it, and I don't dispute it."

He stood in the river with the water rushing around him and the mountain laurels blooming on the bank across the river. For a moment we seemed to be outside of time. He continued, "In a few moments I'm going to put these folk under the water. The water has started on the top of this mountain, and it will sweep over them and wash away all their sins and all their hurts and carry it all down into the ocean of God's forgetfulness. Does anyone else here want to be baptized?" And just for a moment there was a longing that I felt in my breast, like a wild bird beating against a cage. I wanted to have my sins washed away into the ocean of God's forgiveness. I wanted to be blessed. I wanted to come up out of the river like a newborn baby and taste new life and new hope as it dripped off my face. And then I remembered I remembered something that happened before I could remember. I remembered what Martin Luther used to remember, when his life was hard to do and he struggled to go on. I remembered that I had been baptized. That was before I could do anything for myself. When I threw up on myself and someone had to change my diaper and feed me and hold me when I cried, I had been baptized. I am a member of the family of faith and a citizen of the Kingdom of God. And there is nothing in all creation that can separate me from that love.

And that is the word of good news for you today. You have been baptized. You have been recognized and named, and there is a paid-up reservation in your name in one of those rooms that Jesus spoke about when he said, "I go to prepare a place for you."

That doesn't make all the hurt go away. It doesn't make all the dark days bright, or the cancer get well, and it doesn't fix all my problems, but when I hear that—when I remember that I am a child of God and a citizen of his kingdom, regardless of what the world says and regardless of what I have done or failed to do—that makes life not nearly so hard to do.

GREAT EXPECTATIONS

Mark 4:26-34

Did you hear the story about the optimistic fellow who fell off the Empire State Building? As he passed the twenty-fifth floor on the way down, a witness overheard him say, "So far, so good!"

In a day of hopeless headlines, negative news reports, and pessimistic profits, it is clear that we are in need of more optimistic folk. There never seem to be enough men and women who see the glass half-full rather than half-empty. All of us are encouraged when we meet someone who relates to others in terms of possibilities rather than in terms of liabilities. Optimism can be as contagious as pessimism, but what kind of optimism is needed?

When I was a small boy, I would sometimes go to the late afternoon movie and then would have to walk the mile home after it had grown dark. There were times when I was frightened by the sounds I heard and the shadows I saw. To keep my courage up, I whistled. I am not sure what that was supposed to do, but somehow it helped me to feel better, even though it did absolutely nothing to deal with the reality of the noises and the shadows.

The kind of optimism that we need today is not optimism with no more substance than that of a small boy whistling in the dark. It is easy to pretend that all is well and to deny the facts, but what is needed is optimism that is both realistic and hopeful.

The times in which we live are hard on optimism. Just when we felt that peace was breaking out around the world, we see small and brutal wars breaking out on nearly every continent. Just when we thought the nuclear threat had passed, we read of a North Korean government that seems determined to produce nuclear weapons, and we hear about the danger of nuclear weapons created by the former Soviet Union falling into the hands of the Russian Mafia.

A recent graduate of a major university said, "I get to feeling pretty bleak sometimes. I have a sort of apocalyptic view of the world." In a study done at US colleges it was noted that there is a sense among many undergraduates that they are passengers on a sinking ship. In a recent poll taken by Newsweek magazine, 76% of the population thinks that the United States is in a moral and spiritual decline, and 77% blamed this on the breakdown of the family. Some of us may find ourselves feeling like the people who were recently driving down Meeting Street at 2:30 Saturday morning. Just before they passed South Carolina Hall, headed toward the Battery, their car fell into a sinkhole that suddenly appeared. Even the ground on which we stand seems less than dependable.

It is clear that there is a scarcity of optimism in our culture. It is equally clear that there does not seem to be much to support optimism. So, what does one need to have a realistic optimism in a world where much of the evidence suggests that things are not getting better, but maybe getting worse—a lot worse? In the midst of all the bad news, is there any good news that can serve as solid ground on which to build an optimistic outlook?

I don't want to add my voice to the myriad of pessimistic voices in our world today, but the Bible says that if you are putting all your faith and energy into the kingdoms of this world, then you will be disappointed. If you are living a life directed and determined by the wisdom of the age—the wisdom of relativism and self-gratification— then that life will result in frustration, alienation, emptiness, and disappointment. If you are trying to be optimistic about life, but leaving God out of the equation, then your optimism is little more than whistling in the dark.

The good news that comes to us in the word of God is that there is a basis for realistic optimism founded not on the kingdoms of the world or on my craft and cunning, but founded on the promises and power of God. This is what Jesus is speaking about in our Gospel lesson for today.

Jesus lived in a world where there was every reason to be pessimistic. Puppet rulers sat in places of authority. The nation was dominated by pagan, foreign power. Taxes were levied and collected with little opportunity for the taxed to say anything about the taxes. Jesus himself was a person with no earthly power. He had no money backing his ministry and no revolutionary group to do his work in a culture dominated by Rome. In the midst of a world that had every
126

reason to be pessimistic about the future, Jesus was profoundly optimistic. He had great expectations for the future. He gathered a little group of unimpressive men around him and said that they were part of the kingdom of God and that this kingdom was like a mustard seed. It may have a small beginning, but as time goes by, it will grow and develop and become like a great tree.

It may be hard for us to get excited about this, since we live in an age with all sorts of amazing discoveries, but for people living in a prescientific age, it must have truly baffled the mind that something so large could come from something so small.

The parable of the mustard seed is a word of encouragement for us. Things may not be what you and I want them to be, but there is still hope. God works in mysterious ways. God is still with us even when our efforts are frustrated, because he is the source of growth. Growth often starts out small like a mustard seed and then blossoms into something huge.

This gospel lesson reminds me that in order to live optimistically in a world of melancholy, we must be open to hear about some alternative forms of reality. The problem that many people in this country have is that they believe the only way we are going to be fulfilled and have a good life is by *getting* more and more. Life is defined in terms of material success. The kingdom of God is about obedience, about duty to God and others, about living toward a kingdom where there will be no more pain or hurt or tears or darkness or fear. The hope we are called to have is to believe that this kingdom not only will come, but also makes infinitely more sense than the kingdoms that we are now caught up in. Certainly, Abraham must have caught some of the optimism of God when he responded to God's call to leave and go in search of a land that God would show him.

Would you like to live with great optimism and expectation about yourself and about the future? That is what God calls us to have. But in order to have this optimism and these great expectations, we need to be open. First we need to be open to hear.

Nineteen years ago I preached in a little Presbyterian church in Washington, Georgia. In the narthex of that church was a marker commemorating the life of the first pastor. He was, in fact, buried there. The stone marking his grave said, among other things, "Though he is dead, yet shall he speak." One day the caretaker was cleaning in the narthex and read those words. He turned to me and said, "I surely hope he doesn't say anything while I'm in here." Not only do many of us not listen, but also we hope that God doesn't say anything while we are here in church.

But the truth is, if we are going to have hope and expectation, we need to be prepared to listen to God. Some people come to church and don't like what they hear, and go off mad. Some go to sleep and do not listen. God often speaks in a whisper. We listen carefully if we don't want to miss something. If we are going to have hope and great expectations, and live in the light of this hope, we need to listen as individuals and as a church.

And then if we are going to have great expectations and hope about life, we must be open to commitment. Churches are interesting institutions. It dawned on me recently that one of the things that is wrong with this church and is wrong with many churches is that the alumni association is too big. You know colleges have patrons and alumni. If they had no students and faculty, they would be out of business. If you are going to be optimistic about the future and about the kingdom of God that is coming, then you need to get out of the First (Scots) Presbyterian Alumni Association and become an active, participating member. If you want to have great hope and great expectations about the future, then it is important for you to be open to commitment in your life.

When I was very small, I used to go out in the garden that my father planted about this time of year, and I would plant some seeds. My seeds usually didn't sprout because everyday I would dig them up again to see how they were doing. No one really knows what causes a seed to sprout--scientists have been unable to create synthetic seeds and make them grow. Growth is a mystery. Our task is to plant seeds and then to leave them alone and trust God to cause them to sprout and grow. It is often easy for us to lose patience and hope because there seems to be nothing happening. But who knows the results of the seeds we plant?

Several years ago I was a member of the Barium Springs Board of Directors. Their work is with children from hurting homes where the children have never known dependable love. At one meeting we heard about a boy named Tommy. He had come to the Home from a very disturbed situation. The staff had worked with him, they had cared about him and loved him, but after six months Tommy had run away. Someone asked the director, "Did you fail with Tommy?" The director said, "I don't know. I do know that for six months Tommy was loved and cared about in a way that he had never been cared about before. That experience is in his memory. It is a seed that has been planted. Who knows what will become of it?"

Something about that reminds me about the church and of men like Peter, who denied his Lord three times, but the seed had been planted. Who would have thought that from the often-inept disciples, the Gospel message would spread to all corners of the globe? Yet you and I are here today because twenty centuries ago a tiny seed was planted, and God gave the growth. Are there some tiny seeds that you and I could be planting today? Is there someone around you who needs a seed of love or hope or encouragement? Jesus came to tell us of God's great expectations and of God's great plans and hopes for us. Let us believe that good news, and go out and sow a few seeds this week and be instruments of hope and encouragement.

ARE YOU TOO GOOD TO BE HEALED?

II Kings 5:1-14 Psalm 113 II Timothy 2:8-15 Luke 17:11-19

Well, what did you think of the story of Naaman and his miracle dip in the Jordan River?

Naaman was a Syrian who lived over 800 years before the birth of Christ. He was commander of the Syrian army, confidant of the king, and a mighty man of valor, but Naaman was a leper.

The scripture tells us that Naaman heard that there was someone in Israel who could heal him of his disease. Under the protection and encouragement of his king, Naaman goes to Israel and presents himself to the king of Israel with a letter saying that Naaman is there to be healed of his leprosy. Naaman also brings with him a huge gift of money to give to the person who will heal him. The king of Israel is overwhelmed by the request. He is frightened. He believes that the king of Syria is baiting him by asking him to do something that he is unable to do. But Elisha the prophet hears of the king's problem and asks that Naaman be sent to him. The king of Israel is delighted to send Naaman on to Elisha. When Naaman arrives at Elisha's home, Elisha does not come out to meet this terribly important man. Instead he sends a servant with a prescription for healing.

Naaman is instructed to go and bathe in the River Jordan— dip himself seven times—and he will be cured. Initially, Naaman is insulted and angry. He resists the whole notion of bathing in the River Jordan, but his servants convince him to at least try it. He does what Elisha has instructed him to do. To his utter amazement, he is cured. With deep gratitude he returns to Elisha to offer him a valuable gift. Elisha refuses the gift. Naaman then asks if Elisha will give him two mule loads of dirt to take back to Syria so he can make sacrifices to the God of Israel on that part of the land of Israel. He promises Elisha that from that day forth, he will sacrifice only to the God of Israel—and even when he goes with his king to worship the Syrian gods, he will do so asking the God of Israel to forgive him.

On first hearing this lesson from the Old Testament you might have concluded that no more evidence is needed to substantiate the oft-repeated charge that the Christian church is irrelevant to the life most of us lead from Sunday to Sunday. Read with the proper inflections and supplied with the right pauses, this story of Naaman and his miracle dip in the river Jordan might be called interesting, but what in God's name does it have to do with you and me?

Here we are in church. We have come from a variety of experiences to this time and to this place. We have brought with us our memories of experiences from the week just past and our hopes and concerns for the week that is before us. Some of us are sitting here this morning trying to relax and not think about the work at the office or in the classroom. We may still be chafing from some bad encounter with a supervisor, or struggling with how to deal with a subordinate or a peer. Others of us may be worried about a loved one: a brother or sister who is sick; a child who is having a hard time staying on the right road or adjusting to a new situation; a parent whose health and energy is failing. Others of us may simply be struggling with distance between who we say we are and who we really are. We have come to this moment in time bringing with us the stuff that our lives are made of, but I believe it would be safe to say that none of us here has leprosy. I doubt if any of us have ever known anyone with leprosy or even seen anyone with that dread disease. So what does this story of a leper getting cured nearly three thousand years ago have to do with me and with you and the lives that we are living? How do we hear the word of God for me and for you in this story that, on first glance, seems about as relevant to my life and to your life as a repair manual for a covered wagon?

As I sat with this scripture and sifted through it in search of a connection, it finally dawned on me that this story is more than a story about leprosy and washing in the Jordan River. It is really a story about a man who has something the matter with him—and that something is threatening his ability to live the life that he feels called to live. Naaman could well have said the words of Paul: "O wretched man that I am! Who will deliver me from this body of death?" And when I hear that, I begin to see that old Brother Naaman starts to sound like somebody I know.

Naaman is like me and like you in the fact that he has a flaw that is messing up his life. Naaman knows that he has a problem that will eventually destroy him. If you are here today with some nagging sense that you have a problem that is keeping you from being the best that you can be, then it is at that point that you can make a connection with Naaman.

The story of Naaman and Elisha is more than the story of a leper in a far away land and in a long-ago time. The story more than anything else is a story about God. It is about the God who comes to us and meets us in unexpected places and through surprising people. It is about a God who can meet us in the midst of our mundane and ordinary concerns, whether they are concerns about work, or family, or loved ones, or school, or some flaw in our lives that always seems to be interfering with the achievement of our best intentions. God broke into Naaman's life through the witness of a nameless servant girl that had been taken captive by Naaman's army. God spoke to Naaman through Elisha who told him something that he must do in order to find healing and hope. God spoke to Naaman through his servants who persuaded him to be obedient to the directions that he had received. God came to this mighty man of valor through a powerless little girl, through the words of Elisha and through the encouragement of nameless servants. In spite of his lack of religious credentials, in spite of the fact that Naaman was the servant of a foreign king and a worshipper of foreign god, God came to Naaman and offered him healing. This story is, first of all, about the amazing grace of God.

The story is also about resurrection. It is about a man who was trapped in a condition that was literally eating away at his body and would eventually end his life—but through his obedience to the word of the prophet Elisha, Naaman is made new. He dips himself seven times in the muddy and unattractive waters of the river Jordan and he is made whole again. He engages in an act that looks for all the world like baptism. He buries himself in the waters of the Jordan and arises new and different.

The story is about obedience from a man who had wanted his healing to be spectacular and special. He wanted the prophet to come out and pass a mighty miracle in front of God and everyone. But the prophet did not come out. Instead he sent his servant with instructions to do something that Naaman felt was beneath his dignity. Naaman was a powerful, important man. The instructions from the servant of the prophet directed Naaman to do something that he thought would make him a public spectacle. But through the encouragement of his servants, Naaman was obedient to the instruction that he was given. He did what the man of God told him to do, and in the doing of it he was healed.

This story is about the power of God. It is about a God who can heal the hopeless. It is about the love of God that extends beyond the boundaries of the people to whom his love was promised, and reaches out to include those who have no claim on his mercy.

But that is not all the story is about. Stand again before this ancient story and look again at the characters in this little drama. There is Elisha, there is the king of Syria, there is the king of Israel and there is Naaman—but wait, Naaman is more than just a Syrian who lived nearly 3000 years ago. Naaman is you and me.

Naaman is the part of me and of you that longs to be healed of the flaw that separates us from neighbors, from God and from our calling. Naaman is the part of you and me that knows that the good that we should, we do not and the evil that we should not, that we do—and we wish there was some magical way for that to be different. We are like Naaman in that we have received instructions about what we need to be doing. We are to be baptized—dipped in the waters of atonement—we are to be faithful and obedient members of the church, we are to love neighbors as he has loved us, we are to practice forgiveness, we are to pray, we are to be good stewards of what has been entrusted to us, we are to serve God and our neighbors in the places that we find ourselves. It is not that we have no word from the Lord about what we need to do in order to be healed and to move toward wholeness, it is that we often do not like the instructions that we have been given, and we have resisted doing what the Lord has instructed us to do—and in that we are like Naaman who, on hearing that he was to go and dip himself in the river Jordan, said, "I am too important a person to do that. I am too good to engage in that kind of thing."

It should not escape our attention that Naaman had some responsibility for his own healing. He did not do it himself, he did not even know initially what to do, but in the final analysis his healing was tied to the degree to which he was *obedient* to the instructions that he had been given.

Would you like for your life to be different? Would you like the life that you live to be more like the life that God has called you to live? Are you a man or a woman who from time to time finds that you are a leper—a person who is hopelessly flawed and who must confess with the Apostle Paul that the good that you would, you do not and the evil that you would not do, that you do? There are words from the Lord for me and for you. Words that call us to be obedient. Have you followed the instructions that you have been given, or do you think that somehow the instructions that you have received are beneath you, or they are not special enough for you? Are you too good to he healed?

Last week a man came to see me in my office. He is not a member of this church. He wanted to talk to me about a project he is involved in here in the city. In the course of the conversation he told me how he had gotten involved in this project. Up until a couple of years ago his life was a life of selfishness. He cheated his neighbors and cheated on his wife. One day he noticed a small lump in his neck and he finally went to a doctor. After the lump was removed he was told he had cancer. It had spread to other parts of his body. A friend came to see him in the hospital and told him about Jesus. After his friend left he made a decision to surrender his life to Jesus. He told me that the Lord removed from him his hurtful attitude and changed his life. He does not know what his future is as far as his cancer is concerned, but he believes that in the most profound sense, he has been healed. He described the life that he is living now as a life of joy and fullness. In the midst of his illness, this man found his way to the deepest kind of health a man or woman can have.

I wonder how many people back in Syria Naaman told about his dip in the river Jordan? Naaman was cured of more than his illness. He was made whole spiritually.

The word of the Lord to Naaman—to you—and to me—is that God wills our well-being. God desires to make you and me whole. The crucial question is not: Am I good enough to be healed? The crucial question that this lesson poses for us is this: Am I too good to be healed? Am I willing to be obedient to the vision that I have been given? Will I do what I have been told to do? Will I take God at his word and follow his instructions? Naaman was a man whose pride was almost more deadly than his leprosy. His healing was more than skin deep. But it only took place when he was willing to be obedient to the word of the Lord that came to him.

Well, what do you think of the story of Naaman and his miracle dip in the river Jordan? I think it is an important memory in the community of faith and a story that you and I would do well to pay attention to.

GOD'S PRESENCE IN OUR MOMENTS OF CRUCIFIXION

Jeremiah 23:1-6   Luke 23:33-43

Much of life is lived in the meantime. You are probably living in some kind of meantime today. The meantime is the time between what has been and what will be. It is the time spent waiting for things to be different, or to get better, or to get worse. A lot of meantime moments are also moments of crucifixion.

Have you ever experienced a crucifixion moment? It is one of those moments when the forces of darkness, or despair, or evil, or illness seem to be on the verge of speaking the final word. It may be a moment when death seems to have said the final word about someone that you have loved, or someone who has loved you. In the midst of such moments life does not seem fair, and you may wonder if anyone cares, or if God cares, or even if there is a God.

We all have had, or are having, or will have, moments of crucifixion. Your crucifixion moment may have come when you have done all that you could to mend a relationship with a child, or a spouse, or a parent, and nothing helps. Or one day you discover that your spouse or your child is abusing drugs, or contemplating suicide, or has run away, and it feels like crucifixion. A moment of crucifixion may have come for you when you offered yourself for public office and the opposition attacks you and lies about you and all your efforts come to nothing. It may have happened when you followed the directions of your doctor to the letter and endured the chemotherapy, but the cancer has come back. Your moment of crucifixion may have come as you watched a parent disappear with Alzheimer's, and the day comes when your mother or father does not even know you.

As a pastor, I look back over the years of my ministry and remember many crucifixion moments in the lives of folk that I have been privileged to know and love. I remember stillborn babies. I remember broken homes and broken dreams. I remember little children torn from their parents by sudden infant death syndrome. I remember sitting with a young father of four and his wife pregnant with a fifth child, and hearing the results of the biopsy. "It's advanced melanoma. The cancer has spread throughout your body and there is nothing that we can do." Six weeks later I told his children that their father was dead. I remember wondering if God cared. A young mother was killed instantly in a head-on collision with a drunken man. What could I say to her husband or to her children? And I remember early one Easter morning receiving a phone call from a former parishioner, who told me that their eldest son had gone out alone in the night and put a bullet through his head. Moments of great pain, anger, and confusion. Moments in which we often cry out, "My God, my God, why hast thou forsaken me?" In such moments we are often hard pressed not to agree with Shakespeare's Macbeth when he said that life is "a tale told by an idiot, full of sound and fury," but "signifying nothing."

What do you do when such moments happen in your life?

Are you saying, "None of these things have ever happened to me?" That may well be true, but if you live long enough, some of these things will happen to you. That is not a pessimistic statement. It is a realistic statement. The issue that is before us is not how to avoid such moments. We cannot. The issue is how to live in them, and through them, without being utterly defeated by them.

And that is what I want you to think about with me today. What does the Bible have to say about how to live in the moments of crucifixion? If we are faithful to God, will that keep these things from happening? What can we expect? Where is God in these moments when we often seem utterly alone? What is there to sustain us in such moments? What is our responsibility to and for others who are living through moments of crucifixion?

First, let us look briefly at the two passages of scripture from the lectionary.

The first passage is from Jeremiah. It is addressed to a nation that has not been faithful and to leaders who have not led in the way that they should have led. It predicts the exile that will take place, that will come as a result of the people's own unfaithfulness. It says that the people will be punished for the evil that they have done, but that is not the final word. In the midst of the warning there is a word of hope and promise. The promise is for restoration and renewal. The promise is for a savior to come. These people who are about to live through a national moment of crucifixion are told that God will care for them, and they will no longer be afraid, or terrified, and none will be missing. God will not forsake them. God will not forget them. God will bring them back and restore their fortunes.

The gospel lesson is one that is associated with Good Friday. It is the story of crucifixion as told by Luke. Jesus Christ is carried off to be put to death on a cross. He is crucified not because of what he has done, but because of the evil that he has encountered. He has come into a world of sin and darkness to seek and to save the lost, but the world rejects him. It mocks him. It scorns him. It crucifies him. But Luke tells us that he is not crucified alone. Crucified with him are two thieves. One of the thieves mocks him. The other asks for his mercy. Jesus says to him. "Today you will be with me in paradise."

What does this have to say to our questions about moments of crucifixion?

The first thing that it tells us is that our Lord and Savior, Jesus the Christ, understands our moments of crucifixion. He has been there. It was he who felt abandoned on the cross when he cried out, "My God, my God, why hast thou forsaken me?" When he was crucified, all of his friends forsook him and ran away. He was utterly alone. He had done nothing to deserve what happened. His crucifixion took place because his life ran head-on into the sin and darkness of the world. His death is a clear demonstration of the power and persistence of evil in our midst. This one who had done no evil, who had offered himself for you and for me, who came that we might have life and have it abundantly, was nailed to a cross. And there were with him two thieves.

In our moments of crucifixion are we not like the two thieves crucified with Christ? One mocks him and calls on him to save himself and them, too. He speaks for me in my anger, when the crucifying moments come and I do not understand. He speaks for me when the moments of crucifixion leave me hurt and afraid. He is all in me that would demand that God give an accounting to me for what has happened, or is happening, or may happen in the fixture. But there is the other thief. He seems to understand that what is happening has come to him as a result of his own foolishness or failure. He claims no innocence. He demands no accounting. Rather, he asks for mercy of the one who is crucified along with him. For some reason that is beyond my comprehension, he recognizes that Jesus on the cross is indeed the Christ. Could we not say that this thief on the cross—this unnamed man who was being put to death for his wrongdoing—was in fact the first Christian? He was saved by the amazing grace of God. He was not rescued from the cross, but he *was* rescued from having the cross speak the final word about him.

So what should we expect in the living of our days? Should we expect the world to be fair? I would like the world to be fair. I would like it to be like a well-run kindergarten where good is rewarded and evil is punished. But that is not how it is. Bad things do happen to good people, and good things happen to bad people. There seems to be no rhyme or reason to it all. What should we expect? Jesus did not tell his followers that in his fellowship there would be no bad days, or abandonment, or injustice, or rejection, or suffering. In fact, he said just the opposite. He said, "In the world you will have tribulation." Should we expect to be appreciated and understood when we represent the light of Jesus Christ in a world of darkness? We should expect no more than our Lord received. He came unto his own and his own received him not.

We live in a world where all manner of painful things can happen. Many of them are the result of our own failure or the failure of others. We live in a sinful world filled with hurt and pain. The good news is that God, in Jesus Christ, entered that world and experienced that world and promises to redeem that world and to make all things new. He promises a new heaven and a new earth where there will be no pain or suffering or crying—where there will be no moments of crucifixion. He tells us that nothing can separate us from his love. He tells us that no matter how alone we may feel, we are never really or finally alone, for my Jesus and your Jesus has been on a cross, and is able to enter fully into the crucifying experiences that come to men and women in a broken world.

Where is God in our moments our crucifixion? He is with us. He is the one who promised that he would not leave us desolate— like children without parents—but that he would, and does, come to us. He does not abandon us. He did not abandon his people in Egypt living under the oppression of Pharaoh. He did not abandon his people carried off into Babylon in exile. He became flesh and dwelt among us to seek and to save the lost. And when we accept him as our Lord and Savior, he promises to live in us and through us and to give us what we need to live through the crucifying moments of life.

Even in the midst of moments that make no sense and seem to defy any hope we are sustained by his presence. We are sustained by the memory of his crucifixion and by the Easter morning that followed. We are sustained by the presence and memory of a God who can say, "Yes" to all of our "No's."

Years ago I was attending a seminar on prayer at the National Cathedral. The Warden of the College of Preachers, Father Herbert O'Driscoll, was leading the seminar. He spoke of the importance of prayer. He noted that we should pray for those in trouble, and for ourselves, to be sustained and to be faithful. And then a lady in the group raised her hand. He called on her. She recounted a story of moments of crucifixion with an only son who seemed hopelessly addicted to drugs. He had been in treatment programs and nothing seemed to have made any difference. He was estranged from his family and living on the street. "Will you pray for my son?" she asked. What could be said? What prayer could be offered that had not been offered before? Father O'Driscoll paused and then invited us to bow our heads. "Dear Lord, we have heard again about the crucifixion. We wait for Easter."

We are sustained by the memory of Easter and the hope that is given to us by one who promises to make all things new.

And what is our responsibility to those around us who are living their way through some moment of crucifixion? Can we fix the problem? Can we make it go away? We cannot. But there is something we can and are called to do. We are called to be present with folk in the crucifying moments. We are called to sit with them and pray with them and be with them. And it is that presence that can offer them the hope and the strength that they need to live through these moments. As God has not abandoned us, so we are not to abandon one another. As God's children, we are called to represent his love and his mercy. We are called to let the light shine through us and to mediate the grace of Jesus Christ in the dark moments of life.

Years ago while serving as a hospital chaplain, I called on a woman in the psychiatric unit of the hospital. She had a drug-induced psychosis. She was out of control. She was angry. She was abusive to all who entered her room. She screamed at me and cursed me. I listened to her invective. I tried to be present with her. I heard her pain and her hurt, and after a while I prayed for her and left. The next day I went back to see her. She seemed different. She was calm. I noted that she seemed better. She said she was better. She said my visit had turned things around for her. "Why?" I asked. What had I done? "You were the first person," she said, "who did not immediately leave me when I was so ugly and abusive. For the first time I felt that there might be some hope for me."

As Christians we are called to be living reminders of the grace and the love and even of the suffering of our Lord Jesus Christ. Our ministry to one another rests on the conviction that nothing, absolutely nothing, is outside the realm of God's judgment and mercy. The strategy of the principalities and powers of this evil world is to disconnect us from God. When we go and offer ourselves to be with another, we are there to maintain the connection. When we sit with the sick, or weep with the bereaved, or watch with the dying; when we serve a meal at the shelter, or take a meal to someone who is old and alone; when we clothe the naked, or visit the prisoner, or welcome the stranger; when we nurture a little child, or encourage a struggling couple, or listen to a person pour out their hurt and pain; when we do these things, we are living reminders of the one who came to seek and to save the lost. We are living reminders of the one who knows the meaning of crucifixion. We are living reminders of Jesus Christ, and we offer ourselves to maintain the connection that the powers and principalities seek to sever.

What is our task? I often find it summarized in the instructions given by Hamlet to Horatio in the final scene of that play. Hamlet is dying and he speaks to Horatio. "If thou didst ever hold me in thy heart, absent thee from felicity awhile and in this harsh world draw thy breath in pain to tell my story."

Living in the meantime moments of life, we trust the Lord, we tell the story and we wait with hope for Easter.

VISIONS OF FAITHFULNESS: PREVAILING GRACE

Genesis 29:15-28   Psalm 128
Romans 8:26-39   Matthew 13:31; 44-52

Last evening as I stood here in the sanctuary of First Scots Presbyterian Church performing a wedding for two starry-eyed young people, I thought about what a great variety of events are dealt with in the church. There are events of great joy such as weddings, confirmation, and baptisms (like the one we had this morning). But we also come together in this room to deal with great sadness. We pray for the sick and the dying. We gather together to conduct funeral services and assemble in this room in times of national and international crisis and in moments of natural disaster. It is a room where we experience intense joy and happiness. It is also a room where we experience intense sadness, pain and suffering.

But what this means is that what we experience in this room as a community is not unlike what we experience in life. There are good days and bad days. There are moments of great joy amid celebration and heart breaking moments of sadness and hurt. In spite of the fact that much of out culture says we should expect to be happy and life should be filled with excitement, most of us know that is not true.

In his book *The Road Less Traveled*, Scott Peck begins with the statement, "Life is difficult." This is an important truth. One might even say it is an eternal truth. We could add to this statement a number of other truths:
"Life is not fair."
"Things don't always come out even."
"Life often ends before all the loose ends are tied up."

Years ago the writer of Ecclesiastes said some very similar things when he wrote, "The race is not to the swift; nor the battle to the strong; nor riches to the wise; but time and chance happen to us all."

If you have lived very long and have developed any degree of wisdom, you know that this is true. We are not surprised when life is difficult and do not become cynical when life is not fair. And yet in recent years an interesting phenomenon has taken place in our culture. Then has been an emerging notion that life should be fair and should not be difficult. If it is difficult, then it is someone else's fault.

One observer has noted that our culture has become neurotic in that we have done all we can do to avoid pain. We have become a culture of whiners who blame others for whatever there is that is wrong. Our culture and our leaders have not encouraged us to learn how to deal with the pain of life and to take responsibility for out own lives, but have told us that we should do all we can to avoid pain and problems, and if unsuccessful in avoiding these things, then blame others for the problems. That kind of thinking and that kind of living makes us sick. Carl Jung was right when he said, "All neurosis is a substitute for legitimate suffering."

Paul knew of the inevitability of suffering when he wrote to the church at Rome and told them of the prevailing grace of God. "All things work together for good. There is nothing in all of creation that can separate you from the love of God." This is an important passage and one that we need to hear and pay attention to, because it offers us an important word from the Lord about how to deal with, and not be defeated by, the pain and suffering that is a part of our living.

When Paul wrote these words he was focusing primarily on the suffering, the pain, and the hurt that was inflicted on the early Christians as they endured persecution and misunderstanding as a result of their obedience to the call of God. People were being persecuted, tested, hurt, oppressed, and even put to death because of their faith. It would have been easy to conclude that Rome with all of its power would speak the final word and that Rome had the power to put an end to the stories being lived out in the lives of men and women who were seeking to be faithful to God. Paul wanted his brothers and sisters in Rome to know that God would speak the final word.

But I believe that these words are equally helpful to men and women who are experiencing the normal slings and arrows of

143

outrageous fortune. People who have been hurt by life. As one song by Paul Simon goes: "I don't know a soul who has not been battered. . . . I don't know a dream that's not been shattered or driven to its knees."

You may be here today with a broken dream or a broken heart. You may be here driven to your knees by the uncertainty of disease that physicians do not know how to cure. The disease may be in your body or in the body of someone very dear to you. All the evidence that you may be able to assemble at this very moment may cry out for the verdict of "Not Fair!" I don't need to catalogue the slings and arrows of life. Many of you have blessed me by allowing me to walk with you through some of the hard times and the dark days. As much as we may want to, we cannot make the world go away. We do not live in a perfect world. There really is no one to blame for my problems or for yours. What is needed is not to find someone to point to and say, "It is your fault!" What is needed is a way to deal with the hard times and not be destroyed by them.

Years ago I heard about a young couple who became concerned about their young son who always took his teddy bear to bed with him. As the boy got older, they thought he should give this up. Finally they asked him, "Why do you take the teddy bear to bed with you?" Without hesitation he replied, "To have something to hold on to the in the night." I can relate to that. Can you? In the nighttime of our lives we want something to hold on to. I remember the days that I was recovering from open-heart surgery in the hospital. I was having trouble sleeping and would wake up at two or three in the morning and lie in the bed and listen to the sounds of the hospital and listen to the hopes and fears of all my years. I needed something to hold on to in the night. One day a friend came and we had communion together, and I was reminded of these words from the book of Romans: "Nothing can separate you from the love of God." That is something to hold on to in the night.

What happens to you and what happens to me and what happens to those we love is not nearly as important as how we live in response to what happens to us.

An old man was invited to take a ride in a helicopter. He refused and said, "I don't want to do that. Riding in one of those things gets you too close to God." Maybe that's one of the reasons that we are so afraid of the difficult days of life. They bring us closer to God. We can't pretend that we are the masters of our fate and the captains of our souls. We can't pretend that life is something that has no end or no limits. We are faced with our finitude and our mortality, and that gets us closer to God. But what kind of God is it that we get close to?

The words of Paul tell us very clearly. It is a God who has claimed us before we could claim him. It is a God who loved us before we could speak his name. It is a God who will not leave us and who has bound himself to us in a way that nothing can separate. There are no conditions. There are no "if's" in his promise. The relationship that God established with you and with me and with his church is unbreakable. That is something to hold on to in the night.

That life is difficult is perhaps an eternal truth, but the Bible offers some eternal truths that stand over against these truths.

The first truth is that suffering is not meaningless. Look at verse 28 of this eighth chapter. "We know that in everything God works for good." Even in those moments and in those days that seem to make no sense, God is still at work to bring good out of evil. Does that mean that God is the author of broken hearts and broken dreams? By no means. But God's love and God's will is stronger than all the hurts and horrors of life. I believe that God is working for good even when I do not understand or can make no sense out of what has happened. That is something to hold on to in the night!

The second eternal truth is that suffering will not defeat us. In verse 37 we are told, "In all these things we are more than conquerors through him who loved us." Suffering will not finally defeat us as individuals, and it will not defeat us as a church. We can be brave. We can take risks and stand up for what we believe, even though there are lions in the coliseum and some folk may crucify us with their ridicule or with their anger. In spite of what happens or what may happen, we are more than conquerors through him who loved us. Suffering will not defeat us. That is something to hold on to in the night!

The third eternal truth in this passage of scripture is found

145

in verse 38 and 39. "Nothing can separate you from the love of God." It does not say "not many things can separate you from the love of God!" It does not say that normally nothing can separate you. It says simply and unequivocally, "NOTHING can separate you from the love of God!" That is good news. A broken home or a broken life cannot separate you from the love of God. Your past failures and mistakes cannot separate you from the love of God. Old age, broken bodies, cancer, heart disease, depression—none of these can separate you from the love of God. That is good news! That is something to hold on to in the night!

A final eternal truth that is contained in this entire passage is that God's love will not let you go. It will prevail. It will prevail, not because of your faith, or because of your strength, or because of your gritty determination, but because of the love, the faithfulness and the prevailing grace of God.

A chaplain was visiting an old gentleman in the hospital. The old gentleman was dying with a disease that was ravaging his body. Death was leaning on the door. The man told the chaplain what many of us fear in the nighttime moments of our lives. "Chaplain, when it is dark, and I am alone in the early morning hours, and I cannot sleep, I fear that I may lose my hold on God." My friend said, "I understand. But I hope and pray that you will remember that God will not lose his hold on you."

The prevailing grace of God!

That is good news!

That is something to hold on to in the night!

BIBLICAL DIRECTIONS FOR PRAYER

John 3: 19-24   Colossians 1:1 – 14   Luke 11:1-13

The real test of any church is not the size of the budget, or the number of people in attendance, or the number of people on the rolls, but the real test is the number of lives that are being changed.

Anyone who has listened to me for any length of time has probably figured out that one of my favorites verses of scripture is the second verse of the twelfth chapter of Romans. Paul says in this verse, "Do not be conformed to this world, but be transformed by the renewal of your mind, that you may prove what is the will of God, what is good and acceptable and perfect." The church should be a place where transformation is taking place, but in far too many cases that is not true. In fact, one of the biggest problems we have in the church is that we have allowed the world to press us into its mold and thereby have failed to experience the transforming power of the gospel. Instead of looking to the God who created the heavens and the earth for direction and power, we frequently look instead to the wisdom of the world. Instead of receiving the glorious freedom and abundant life of the children of God, we become trapped in all manner of things that lead not to life but to death. Instead of bearing the fruit of righteousness, too often the fruit of our lives is broken dreams, broken promises, and broken lives.

I want you to do a little personal inventory this morning. Ask yourself: "Have I grown in my relationship with God over the past year? Have I received the abundant life that is promised to those who accept Christ as their Lord and Savior? Am I dying more and more to sin and living more to righteousness? Am I growing in my knowledge of the will of God? Is my life a life that bears fruit for God? If not, why not?"

Why do so many folk who claim to have accepted Jesus Christ as Lord and Savior allow themselves to be conformed to this world? What are they failing to do that allows this to happen? What is the difference between those people whose lives give evidence of being transformed and those whose lives give evidence that they are conformed to the world? Why do so many people fail to experience what the scriptures promise?

The answer to that question is found in the second half of the second verse of the fourth chapter of James. It says very simply, "You do not have because you do not ask." You do not receive because you do not pray.

As your pastor, I know that many of you are growing and are bearing fruit for God. I know that many of you are growing in the knowledge of God's will. When I talk with these folk about this growth that is taking place, there is one thing that all of them seem to have in common. They pray. Regular, disciplined prayer is an important part of their lives. They have because they have asked. If you do not have, it is probably because you have not asked.

And that is what I want to talk with you about this morning. I want us to look at some things that the Bible has to say about prayer. The Bible has so much to say about prayer that I could probably preach a sermon on prayer every Sunday for years, so I don't think we are going to cover it all. It is clear, however, from the study of the Bible, that the most powerful privilege that God has given us is the privilege of prayer. And yet prayer is the most underutilized source of spiritual power in the church today.

Let's begin.

What we believe about God will determine what we believe about prayer, how we pray, and even if we pray. If you believe that God is an impersonal presence in the universe who is going to do what he does regardless of anything you might say or do, or if you believe that God is an unmoved mover and an uncaused cause, then it really does not make much sense to pray. But that is not what the Bible teaches us about God. The Bible says that God cares about you. It tells us that even the hairs of your head are numbered. It tells us that God wants to have a relationship with you. It tells us that God came in the person of Jesus Christ to seek and to save you. He came to bring you home. The Bible tells us that when we accept Jesus as our personal savior, we become members of the family of God and citizens of the Kingdom of Heaven.

God wants you to communicate with him. Jesus said to his disciples that they could come to God and call him father. What would it say about your relationship with your own father if you said that you recognize him as your father, but you will never talk to him, or that you believe that he really won't do anything to help you in time of trouble? Jesus instructed his disciples to ask, and it would be given to them; to seek, and they would find; to knock, and the door would be opened. Does that sound like a God who is an unmoved mover or an uncaused cause? By no means! Jesus is speaking of a God who loves you and wants to have a relationship with you, who has gone the second and third and fourth mile to make that happen. Do you want to grow? Do you want to be transformed? Do you want your home to be a place where God's love is present? Do you want to bear fruit for the kingdom of God? Then ask. Ask and you shall receive. Come to God in prayer.

But you may be saying, "I really don't know what to pray for. How do I know that what I pray for will be the will of God?" In the lessons that I have read this morning there are two prayers. One is in the gospel lesson and the other in the reading from Colossians. If you pray either one of these prayers, there is no need to end it with "If it be your will." What you are asking for in these prayers *is* the will of God.

If you want to pray a prayer that will change you and change those around you, then I commend to you this prayer from the book of Colossians. It begins in verse nine of the first chapter and is a prayer that Paul prayed constantly for the Colossians. If you pray this prayer every day, then two things will happen. The person you pray for will be changed—maybe not immediately, but eventually—and you will be changed. It is a prayer you can pray for others and a prayer you can pray for yourself. It is certainly a prayer you can and should pray for your spouse, for your children, for your siblings, for your parents, and for the leaders in the church. If you don't want to be changed, then don't pray this prayer, because if you do, things will happen.

Listen to the prayer that Paul prays: "We have not ceased to pray for you, asking that you may be filled with the knowledge of his will in all spiritual wisdom and understanding, to lead a life worthy of the Lord, fully pleasing to him, bearing fruit in every good work and increasing in the knowledge of God. May you be strengthened with all power, according to his glorious might, for all endurance and patience with joy, giving thanks to the Father, who has qualified us to share in the inheritance of the saints in light."

This is a good prayer. It is prayer that works, and I know it works because it has worked for me. Will it work if we pray it only one time? No. The first thing that I want you to notice is that this is a prayer that Paul said he prayed continuously. He said, "We have not ceased to pray for you." It is not a prayer to be prayed once or from time to time. Rather, it is a prayer to be prayed every day. If you can't remember it, it is written out in the Bible. You can read it as your prayer. Second, it is a God-centered prayer and not a materialistic wish list, or a prayer to get you out of a problem. It does not ask for a new car, or a new spouse, or an "A" on an exam that you have not studied for, or even for a new body. It is God-centered. And, finally, it is a very specific prayer. Frequently when we pray for loved ones we are lazy and we say something like, "Lord, just bless old So-and-So." What do you want the Lord to do? How do you want the Lord to bless them? What do you want the Lord to do for your children, or for your friends, or for you? This prayer is very specific.

Now, what is the first thing that we should pray for? We pray first to be filled with knowledge of God's will in all spiritual wisdom and understanding. We come to God and ask first of all to know the will of God. We ask to be filled with this knowledge. We want to know what God is up to and if we are living in accordance with his will. We ask God first of all to show us his will for our lives. Let me warn you about one thing. Some people, when they pray, get stuck in their own past. They begin to believe that God will not fulfill his promises in them because their past is so bad or their sins so many. Know this. The past is important to psychotherapists, but it is not important to God. God says, "I am interested not so much in what you have been, but in what you can become. The past is forgiven. The past is history. I am a God who can make all things new."

The second thing that we pray for is to lead a life worthy of the Lord, and a life that is fully pleasing to him. What we are saying to God is that as a child of God we want to lead a life that God will be proud of and that will be pleasing to God. We want our

150

real family to be proud of us. We don't want to do anything that will bring dishonor to our real family. This means that we are asking that God keep us from being conformed to the world. We are asking that we not be seduced into believing that what the world thinks of us and says about us is more important than what God thinks of us. You remember that Jesus said, "Woe to you when all men speak well of you." If your life is no threat to the powers and principalities of darkness in the world, and the powers and principalities of darkness all say what a wonderful, nice person you are, then you have missed the point of what it means to be children of the light and not of the darkness. The world did not have much good to say about Jesus. In fact, in the final analysis, the world was so upset with him that he was crucified. Did you know that there are more Christian martyrs today than at any other time in history—men and women the world does not speak well of? Let us pray that as individuals and as a church we will live a life worthy of our calling.

The third thing that we pray for in this prayer is that we bear fruit in every good work. Now let me make one thing crystal clear. All of us bear fruit. The issue is not whether we bear fruit or not. The issue is the kind of fruit we bear. The kind of fruit we bear is determined by what is planted and nurtured at the center of our lives. If you have planted greed, or jealousy, or criticism, or anger, or selfishness, then you will bear the fruit of these things. This is not the fruit of righteousness, but is a fruit that is destructive and poisonous and rotten. This prayer is asking that our lives make a positive and eternal difference. What kind of fruit is being borne in your life? What kind of difference will your life have made when it is over? Will you be remembered as someone who has made a positive and eternal difference in the lives of those around you? Let me give you one warning about this part of this prayer. If you pray that God will let you bear fruit and then you are given an opportunity to bear fruit, do not say "Lord, that is not quite what I had in mind." God may give you things to do and ways to bear fruit that may challenge you and stretch you.

Then you ask God to strengthen you with all power, according to his glorious might. When you were baptized, God placed his Holy Spirit in you. God came to live in you, and you have all the power that you need to do what you are praying for. When you pray this prayer, you are asking God to release in you and nurture in you what is already there. When you pray this for your children, you are praying for God to nurture and release what is already there. For some of us, the spirit in us is like a seed that has never germinated. This prayer is like watering the seed. You have what you need to do and to be what God wants you to do and to be. This prayer will nurture that and release it.

And finally, you are to pray for endurance and patience. We pray that God will give us the gift of patience and stick-to-it-ness. This is not a prayer that you pray once and then quit if nothing seems to happen. We don't stop praying and turn away from God because he gives us something that is not what we expected or because it appears that the prayer is not working. One of the signs of immaturity in people is the need for instant gratification and an inability to endure in order to complete a task or reach a goal. The same is true for immature Christians. If you want to receive the blessing that God has for you, and if you want to bear fruit, and if you want others for whom you pray to bear the fruit of righteousness, then you need to hang in there. Remember the words of Winston Churchill who spoke to a group of boys in a British prep school. His word to them was: "Never, never give up!" Ask God to give you endurance.

One last word. Do I pray this prayer just for people that I care about and who care about me? No. This is an especially good prayer to pray for those who appear to be living in darkness. It is a good prayer to pray for your enemies. Not only can God change you and those you love, but God can change them, too.

The real test of any church is not the size of the budget, or the number of people in attendance, or the number of members on the church roll, but the real test is the number of lives that are being changed. If you want to be changed, then ask and you shall receive, seek and you shall find, knock and it shall be opened to you.

HAS THE WORLD GOT YOU DOWN?

Luke 17:5-10

Do you find that there are some things in the Bible that you really like and others that you wish were not there? I do. I like the parts that speak of grace and mercy. I like the stories that tell me that God is kind and forgiving. I especially like the story of the prodigal son. This irresponsible son comes home broke and in rags after making a mess of his life. What does the father do? Does he punish him or lecture him? No! He rushes out to greet him. He hugs him. He puts a ring on his finger. He gives him new clothes and new shoes. He has a party to welcome him home. The Bible says that God is like this and loves us the way this father loves the bad son. I like that. I like it because I see myself being like the bad son sometimes. Every now and then I want to wander into some far country and do things my way. I say things like "I want to find myself." But I always seem to end up making a mess of things and having to come home. The self I end up finding is not one that I like very much. I like knowing that God will love me and welcome me when I come back home. I like it when the Bible says that while we were sinners, Christ died for us. I like all these stories about Jesus coming to seek and to save the lost, because I feel lost at times. I like the 55th chapter of Isaiah. The people living in exile are invited to come home. They are assured that they are forgiven even if they have been disobedient. I like that. I like knowing that God loves me in spite of what I have done or failed to do.

I just wish that were what the entire Bible said.

Just when I start to feel really comfortable, the Bible starts talking about obedience.

Obedience means that I am supposed to do what God tells me to do. To be obedient means that I do it God's way and not my way. To be obedient means that I look to God for direction. To be obedient means that I don't make up my rules, but follow God's rules. To be obedient means doing the right thing as God has defined the right thing. I don't get to make up what is right.

On the face of it, that sounds O.K. God gives the directions; I follow them. Nothing to that, until I begin to read what God expects. Jesus says that God wants me to do things like turn the other cheek; be generous with my possessions; love my enemies; pray for those who hurt me; love God more than I love my family; be willing to give up my life in obedient service to God; be more concerned about others than I am about myself; don't live by the rules of the world but live by God's rules. And to make it even more difficult, I am reminded that God expects me to feed the hungry; care about the poor and the powerless; take care of the environment; be a peacemaker in a world weary of war.

When I hear all of that I begin to feel like the man who heard the preacher telling him to love his neighbor as he loves himself. He responded: "Those are mighty fine words, preacher, but what if it just ain't in you to do it?" Sometimes the distance between what we are and what we should be is so great that we just get stuck. When I hear about all the things that God expects me to do, I feel overwhelmed. It gets me down. It doesn't seem like it is in me to do it. And when I feel this way, I often just get stuck. Sometimes I get so stuck that I don't do anything at all.

And it is not just the stuff in the Bible about love and forgiveness and doing the right thing that gets me down. Lots of times the problems in the world get me down. Last week I talked about problems in the world as we celebrated worldwide communion. There are many problems. We hear about them every day. We see them in our newspapers and on television. We see pictures of people blown apart in Eastern Europe. We see pictures of folk who have no homes and no food. We hear about global warming and the greenhouse effect. We read of the increasing crime in our inner cities. In the midst of all of these reminders we come to church and hear that our response should be "Here am I Lord, send me." Does that ever get you down?

Last week someone said to me after the service, "All of that stuff about the needs of people gets me down. What I need help with is in celebrating and feeling hopeful. I often come to church with an ounce of joy and a pound of depression. I need to find a lot of joy in the worship service because joy is what I find so difficult to find in the world."

I know that feeling. I used to watch the news every morning while I was getting dressed. I soon discovered that I could not deal with what tie to wear and the revolution in Bosnia. I couldn't listen to the news about men and women starving or being murdered in some faraway place and enjoy my breakfast. The world had me down.

The problems of the world get us down, but the problems of life also get us down. Sometimes it is all we can do to get through the day. God tells me to be obedient, but I have a child who is dreadfully sick. God tells me to love my neighbor, but I can't even love the people I live with. I am told to rejoice in the Lord, but if it wasn't for Prozac, I might not even get up in the morning. God says to be generous but it is all that I can do just to pay my bills.

Has the world got you down today? Are you more aware of your pain than of your joy? Are you more aware of your hurt than of any healing in your life?

Are you more aware of your emptiness than of your fullness? Are you more in touch with your anger than with your forgiveness? Are you more aware of your powerlessness than of your ability to being about any real change? Are you so aware of all these things that you feel stuck?

Perhaps it was something like this that the disciples felt when Jesus told them that they were to forgive someone as many as seven times in a single day. The disciples were trying to do the right thing, but it was not easy. They had left their jobs, their families, and their friends. They listened to Jesus' parables that they often did not understand. They saw him spend hours healing the sick and teaching great crowds when they felt bone-tired and sick of people. When they saw him perform miracles they must have thought, "I can't do that." Telling them to forgive someone seven times in a single day may have been something of a last straw. And it must have been out of a sense of deep inadequacy that they said to Jesus, "Increase our faith." They thought they just didn't have what it would take to do all this forgiving business.

The thing that is really interesting in this lesson is what Jesus did not tell them and what he did tell them.

He did not give them ten easy steps to increase their faith. He did not start a class on increasing your faith. He did not offer them a home study course or give them a book to read or tell them to go and spend time alone praying for more faith. He did not suggest that he have a private counseling session with each of them to explore how their family history might have impacted their faith journey. He didn't say, "Don't worry about this because I know that it is not in you to do it."

What did he tell them to do? What is the word for us when the world has us down and we feel like we are being asked to do more than we can? Jesus says first that the disciples, and we, are to utilize the faith we have, no matter how small it is. We do not feel our way into a new way of acting. Rather, we are to act our way into a new way of feeling. The real point in all of this is not the amount of faith we have. It is not our faithfulness that matters. It is the faithfulness of God. Great is *his* faithfulness. And when we take our little measure of faith and join it with God's faithfulness, then great things can be accomplished.

When the world gets us down, we often do what the disciples did. When the instructions of Jesus got to be more than they thought they could handle, they focused their attention—where? On themselves. And that was the wrong place to focus. Jesus said to focus on the task. Get on with it. Do the best you can. Love as best you can. Forgive as best you can. Offer what you have and God will give you what you need. Stop thinking about your inadequacy. Stop thinking about your failures and your weaknesses, and focus your attention on God's faithfulness and on God's victory.

A minister approached a man about joining the church and the man said he did not want to join. His reason? There were too many hypocrites in the church. The minister responded, "There is always room for one more."

You are right. It *isn't* in you to do it. But God, working in you and through you, can do it. Use the faith you have—no matter how small. When you use the faith you already have. you will stop saying to yourself things like, "It can't be done," or "One person can't make a difference." Faith cancels out words like *impossible, preposterous,* and *absurd.* As Gordon Cosby of the Church of the Savior has said, "Just because something seems impossible is no reason not to try to do it."

Have any of you heard of Mary McLeod Bethune? She was born in Mayesville, S.C. in 1875. She was one of 17 children born to a family of freed slaves living on a plantation in Mayesville. When she was nine years old she could not read or write. When she was eleven she went to a mission school and then went to the Moody Bible Institute in Chicago. After finishing Moody Bible Institute she returned to the south to start a school for black girls from Florida. When she started the school she had $1.50. Less than a grain of mustard seed. She baked pies and sold them to tourists to get the money to keep the school going. Her school became Bethune-Cookman College and Mary became president. Later she helped Franklin D. Roosevelt start the National Youth Administration. Mary McLeod Bethune did not let the world get her down. She took the tiny little bit she had and used it, and great things happened.

Even small amounts of faith can accomplish great things. Jesus is not reprimanding his disciples for having so little faith. He is affirming them for the faith they have. A little bit of faith goes a long way.

Don't let the world keep you down. You can make a difference. You can do it better this week than you did last week. There are lots of things in the world that seem to be beyond my capacity to touch, but what about the things that are right in front of us that we can touch? John F. Kennedy understood this when he said, "Maybe we cannot keep all the children in the world from starving, but we can keep one child from starving." Maybe we cannot solve the problems of all the homeless in the world, but by supporting our local shelter we can give folk a place to stay tonight who would not have had one. Beware of being so wiped out by what is happening in some land far away that we fail to see and respond to opportunities we have to be faithful right here in Charleston. I would like to see us, here at this church, to begin to do what we can to build bridges between this church and others in the community. I would like to see us reach out more intentionally to our black brothers and sisters in Charleston and especially to two of our neighboring Presbyterian churches on the peninsula that are predominantly African American.

To live by faith means that we take God more seriously than we take our inadequacy and lack of faith. To live by faith means that we recognize that you and I have not been called to be the Lord of history. Rather, we have been called to be servants in the movement of history. The outcome of history is in the Lord's hands. Our efforts cannot bring in the kingdom, but we can participate in its arrival. We cannot solve all the problems of the world, but we can be a part of some small victories over evil and suffering. Our joy and our hope are not rooted in our goodness or our faithfulness or our ability to do what we have been told or to be obedient. Our joy and our hope are rooted in God—the God who made the heaven and earth. The God who came in the person of Jesus Christ to seek and to save the lost. The God who came in the person of Jesus to offer himself on the cross for my sins and for yours—to rescue us from our inability to be obedient. So, when the world gets you down—when you think that you have been asked to do more than you are able to do—do this: do the best that you can. Use the faith that you have. Offer what you have to Jesus, remembering that Jesus is Lord. He will speak the final word. He has been Lord from the beginning. He will be Lord at the end, and even now he is Lord.

God's Guest List: Meeting Yourself Again For The First Time

Luke 13:22-30

If you were asked to paint a picture of yourself, what kind of picture would you paint? What kind of information would you use to paint that picture? Would the emphasis in that picture be on what is good and helpful, or would it be on what is wrong? Unfortunately, many, if not most of us, are surrounded by folk who seem to have no difficulty pointing out our defects, but who seem unable to see or acknowledge our assets, our potential, and our possibilities. Parents worry about the self-esteem of a child but do not seem to know or remember that the way a child feels about herself is directly related to how the most important person in the child's life feels about her. If that child is a source of delight and is cherished, then it is almost a certainty that the child will be a delightful child. I have never known a child who was spoiled by getting too much love. On the other hand, if the message read in the face of the parent is a message of disapproval and judgment, the child is likely to grow up feeling both judged and judgmental.

A therapist friend of mine in Western North Carolina reminded me recently that the picture we paint of ourselves is painted with the information or the feedback we receive from the people around us. The information that carries the most weight tends to be the information we receive from the people we live with and the people who are most important to us. And even if the information we receive from these people is inaccurate, we still use that information to paint the picture, and sometimes the picture we paint of ourselves doesn't look anything like the person that we are. The point of this is that we have a very important role to play in how folk around us think of themselves and feel about themselves. The second point is that how you may feel about and think about yourself may be based on very inaccurate data that you have received from someone close to you and important to you.

Have you ever noticed that some children grow up thinking that they are capable of doing wonderful things, that they have great potential? And have you noticed that there are many folk who spend a great deal of their life trying to overcome a long-term, negative message they received from someone close and important to them? When I worked as a therapist, I saw people whose lives were profoundly impaired because they had seen in the eyes of their parents and heard in the voices of their parents words of judgment, anger, and condemnation. The two most important people in their life let them know that they did not like them, and, therefore, it was all but impossible for them to like themselves.

In his best-selling book *Care of the Soul,* Thomas Moore comments on the notion that "love is blind," and suggests that instead of being blind, perhaps love is really the capacity to see in another person what is wonderful and good about the person. Love looks beyond and through the obvious defects and sees the good and the wonderful. To have someone know you through and through and love you still and all is a powerful and energizing thing. Such folk are the most important people in our lives.

The Bible tells us that Jesus Christ was and is this kind of person. He knows us through and through and loves us still and all. I am convinced that when we meet the real Jesus, we meet ourselves again for the first time, because he looks at us with the eyes of love and listens with the ears of acceptance.

And it was precisely this characteristic that made him so offensive to the Pharisees. Jesus challenged the way his culture valued or devalued people. The Pharisees were sort of the equivalent of the religious right of Jesus' day. They seemed to know more about God than God did. They were sure about everything that they believed and taught, and those who disagreed with them were viewed as dangerous and should be silenced. The Pharisees were the rule-makers and rule-enforcers. They had worked hard to create a society that could identify the folk who were unacceptable because they did not or could not keep the rules and the requirements of this rigid and legalistic system.

One of the images used in the Bible to describe those who would be acceptable in the end-time—and, by implication, who is acceptable in the now time—was to talk about the messianic banquet. This messianic banquet was a great party that would take place at the end of history when the Messiah and the holy angels would come and destroy the forces of sin and darkness in a holy war. Following the battle there would be this great feast where certain worthy folk would be included. The Pharisees figured that they knew who was going to be invited to the party and that their names would be at the head of the list. Completely absent from the guest list would be foreigners, folk who did not keep the law, the sick, the lame, the deformed, the blind and the deaf. According to the Pharisees, history was moving toward a climax in which their worldview would be certified as correct. The messianic banquet would have a guest list that would include only those folk that they said were OK, and would not include any folk that they said were not OK. Their position was not unlike a friend who said that he had this fantasy when he and his wife were having an argument. He imagined that there would be a knock on the door and he would open the door. There would be an angel there who would say to my friend, "Henry, you are right! Mary, you are wrong!"

The really offensive thing that Jesus said, as far as the Pharisees were concerned, was that God might have a guest list that was very different from the one they imagined. In fact, Jesus suggests that the Pharisees may have a hard time getting a seat themselves, and then goes on to say that people will come from north and south and east and west (which was a Hebrew way of saying that they would come from everywhere) and sit down at the table in the kingdom of God, and the first will be last and the last will be first. There will be folk there who had no idea that they would be included in the guest list—people who fed the hungry and clothed the naked and welcomed the stranger and visited the prisoner. To put it in today's vernacular, we could hear Jesus say that there will included at the banquet, those who are failures and those who appear to be misfits—white trash, and chronically unemployed black single mothers, gay people, drug users. We do not know for sure who will be included, but Jesus said that those who will be on the guest list will be all of those folk who God, in his great mercy, chooses, and the way God chooses may have absolutely nothing to do with the way we choose or value people.

Now what does this mean for us? I think we find in the ministry and teaching of Jesus (and we are reminded of this in this passage) some very important clues to what it means to be the people God intended us to be. We find some important clues about what it means to be the church of Jesus Christ. I want to mention three things that I hope you will take away with you this morning.

The first is to beware of the Pharisees. One of the things that we learn in our theological tradition is the importance of being sure, but the danger of being too sure. There are a number of things that I am sure about, but I am not nearly so sure of my interpretation of those things. I am sure that God is with us, but I am not always sure what that means or how that looks. I am sure that what we do matters, but I am not sure that I know, among the many things we do each day, which of them is really important. I believe the Bible is the Word of God, but I am not at all sure that I can interpret it correctly. I tell you and me to beware of the Pharisees, but I am not sure that there are not times when I am as judgmental and small-minded as the Pharisees ever were. People who are too sure about anything may be dangerous—and I am pretty sure about that. Beware of the Pharisee. The Pharisee looks at folk, not with the eyes of love, but with the eyes of judgment. The Pharisee is not open to new possibilities, but is seeking to develop a closed system that is free of any anxiety that may be caused by ambiguity.

You will know that you are with a Pharisee when you find yourself feeling worse about yourself, or when you feel or are told that you should be ashamed of yourself. Last week I was with an old acquaintance of mine, and I shared some things I was struggling with and the message I got was that I shouldn't feel the way I did and shouldn't think the things I think. As a result of that encounter, I did not feel better about myself—about the self that God had created— but instead I felt worse about this self. Pharisees have poor vision— they look at the world with judgment, and they have poor hearing, and they do not listen with acceptance. When we meet a Pharisee we introduced to things in ourselves that are not good for others.

On the other had, when we meet Jesus, we meet ourselves for the first time. When Jesus met Peter, an impulsive, simple fisherman, he said "Come with me and you can be a fisher of men." When he went to lunch at the home of Zacchaeus and was criticized by the Pharisees because he was a tax collector, he said, "This man too is a son of Abraham." When the Pharisees brought to him a woman taken in the act of adultery and demanded that she be stoned, he invited those who were without sin to cast the first stone. When Peter failed Jesus and denied him three times, Jesus' faith in Peter never wavered.

162

When you meet Jesus, you meet your real self, perhaps for the first time. Unfortunately, our churches have been infiltrated with Pharisees and Phariseeism, and we come and feel as John Powell did when he wrote his little book, *Why Am I Afraid to Tell You Who I Am?* Powell answered his question by saying, "I am afraid because if I tell you who I am, you might not like who I am, and it's all I've got." Beware of the Pharisee around you and beware of the Pharisee in you.

The second thing I want to remind you and me of is that we live in a world that seems to erode what is best in us and instead nurtures the worst in us. In spite of our technological sophistication and what we call a rising standard of living, rates of depression have been doubling in some industrialized countries every ten years. The three most common causes of death among young adults in North America are car wrecks, homicide, and suicide. E. A. Robinson could have been writing about our time when he said, "The world is a kind of spiritual kindergarten where millions of children are trying to spell God with the wrong blocks." And there are many in our time, especially younger folk, who would agree with A. E. Housman, who wrote, "I am a stranger and afraid/ In a world I never made." People today desperately need to be encouraged. People today need to be acknowledged as important and valuable, because a great many folk feel worthless and unimportant. I believe that the church of Jesus Christ is called today, particularly, to a ministry of encouragement. Someone told me the other day that they were not sure what I meant when I said "ministry." I mean a special activity done in service to others. You can serve your neighbor and love your neighbor by encouraging your neighbor. Think about it wherever you go. Let me make a suggestion to you of one way to do this. Everywhere we go, the people who wait on us wear a nametag. Look at that nametag and when you thank that person, call him or her by name. Acknowledge that you are in the presence of a unique human being. That is encouraging.

And finally, I said earlier that the picture we paint of ourselves is painted with information we receive from someone who is very important to us. Let me remind you of something that you may not know or may have forgotten. Jesus is the most important person in your life, and he likes you. He believes in you. He sees in you great possibility. When we meet Jesus, we meet our real self for the first time, because he looks at us with the eyes of love and hears us with the ears of acceptance. And when that happens, we suddenly begin to have the energy to do the things that Jesus believes we can do. When you became a Christian you asked Jesus to come and live in you. One of the ways you can know that he is living in you is when you are able to see people with the eyes of Jesus, and love them with the heart of Jesus, and hear them with the ears of Jesus. I can do that sometimes. This week I met my youngest granddaughter for the first time. A warm, soft, wonderful little baby named Natalie. When I saw her the first time, she was in a crib in my daughter's room, and I went and leaned down and kissed her on the head and said "Natalie, you are wonderful little girl, and I am so glad you are here." Bless somebody today. Encourage somebody today. Try to catch your spouse or your children or your friends and neighbors or even the clerk at the store or the waitress at the restaurant doing something right, and tell them about it, and you will have made the world a little better, and you will be blessed in the doing of it.

Years ago my supervisor for my counseling training said to me, "Hugh, if you are going to work with a person as a therapist, you must find something about that person that you like and enjoy, or you will never be able to help that person." That is true in counseling, and it is true in life. When you meet others today, say a word of blessing to them. Look for the image of God in them, and see them with the eyes of Jesus, and love them with the heart of Jesus. And when you do that, some of these folk will not only meet Jesus for the first time, but they will meet themselves for the first time.

JESUS AND THE STORMS OF LIFE

Mark 4:35-41

The story from the gospel for today is told with great economy and consumes only six verses. It is tucked in between the parable of the mustard seed, which tells of the kingdom which finds its beginning in the germination of a tiny seed, and the story of a demoniac who struggled with a hellish storm within himself that was calmed by the soothing words of Jesus.

It was evening. Jesus had been with the crowds all day. Now he invited friends to go with him to the other side of the lake—to the sparsely settled eastern shore, to the Golan Heights.

They set sail for the other side. Jesus is bone-weary from the demands of so many people. As the ship begins to settle into the journey, he lies down in the stern with his head upon a cushion and falls asleep.

But the calmness of the journey does not last. A wind springs up. The waves grow with the winds. The ship is battered by the wind and waves. There is a clamor in the boat as sails are adjusted and men do what they can to make the ship secure in the rising storm, but still he sleeps. The rain falls. The men begin to feel uneasy. The ship creeps and labors in the heaving sea, but still he sleeps.

There are times when God seems to be asleep. At first we can cope with the problems that come upon us. We can row well in the calm. The problems are troublesome, but not devastating, until one day something happens that was not anticipated. A phone call comes in the night and tells us that a parent is dead. The doctor calls and tells us that we need to come and talk about the biopsy. It is cancer. A child runs away. A job is lost. A marriage ends. Somewhere deep within, the seeds of fear begin to germinate, and the first leaves of terror break through the calm that has heretofore characterized our lives. In those moments when the unthinkable happens, we look over our shoulder to see where God is and often see no evidence of his presence. Where is he now when we need him so desperately? Is he asleep?

The storm blows and still he sleeps.

The disciples labor to hold the ship steady, but the wind and the waves seem to be more than they can manage. Water crashes over the bow. They adjust the sails again, but still to no avail. They now stand ankle deep in water. The ship begins to wallow in the trough of the waves.

And still he sleeps.

Finally, the tension of the storm and the fear that grips their hearts drives them to act. They call out to him in anger. "Do you not care if we die? How can you sleep in such a storm? Does it not matter to you that the ship and all of us are about to sink beneath the waves? Do you not care?"

In hospital rooms we cry out: "Do you not care?" We see pictures of murdered people in Rwanda and ask: "Does God not care?" We pass a bewildered homeless man on the streets of Charleston, and we wonder: "Does God care if they, or you, or I perish? Does he care?" We feel guilty about our anger and our questions, but we understand and identify with the words of the Psalmist when he cried out, "How long, O Lord? Wilt thou forget me forever? How long wilt thou hide thy face from me?"

And finally they awaken him. He sees their fear and the situation that confronts them. He rebukes the wind and says to the sea, "Peace! Be still!" The wind calms, and the waves grow still. Then he turns to these frightened men, now captured by a different kind of fear, and says to them: "Why are you afraid? Have you no faith?"

Often it is only after we cry out to God—shake our fists at the heavens and accuse him of not caring—only after we have done all the things that frail human beings do when they are afraid—only then do we find our way to a calmness that leads to that introspective moment when we hear him ask about our faith and our fear.

Can you recall some moment in your own experience when he has calmed the stormy seas of your life after you have lashed out at him in fear and anger, accusing him of not caring if you lived or died? How did he do it? It is a mystery that leaves us wondering, and with

166

that wondering often comes another kind of fear: the fear that we are told in the Old Testament "is the beginning of wisdom."

Who is this that walks into the dark center of the human condition and leaves behind a perfect calm and peace that passes all understanding? What has he to do with us in the midst of storms that threaten our lives, shatter our confidence, and leave us wondering if there is anyone who cares what happens to us? Does this story represent a childlike home for a magical God? Or does this story recall the way that God always works?

My reading of the scripture tells me that this is the way God works. This is what we have heard and seen him do. This is what we can expect him to do in the future. In Jesus we find the same power that brooded over the waters at creation, dividing light and darkness, water and dry land, bringing order out of chaos. This is the way God works. We find in Jesus the power of God that brought a slave people to the shores of the Red Sea, and then divided the waters so they could pass through to freedom and to safety. In Jesus we see the same power that invited Noah to build an ark to rescue him and others from the flood that would cover the earth. This is the way God does things. He stills the storm. He brings water to desert places. He leads us through the valley of the shadow of death. He does not forsake us.

And that finally is the good news that we are invited to remember and believe. The good news that the storms of life are powerless over us. The good news is that we cannot be separated by fragile faith, or fear, or anger, or tragedy, or sickness, or anything else in all creation.

"Do you care?" we continue to ask. The answer comes back like an echo: "Yes, I care! I care with a love that is larger than the chaos, greater than the power of the storms of adversity, stronger than your failure or your death. It is a love that will not let you go."

"Who is this man?"

That is the question that each of us must answer. Mark has told us what he has seen and heard: He does not forsake his own. He stills the storm. He brings peace.

But, finally, you must answer the question that faced the disciples: "Who then is this, that even wind and sea obey him?" Who is he for you? Will you trust him in the storms of your life? Will you go with him on the journey that he called you to take? Will you allow him to guide your life and direct your ways? Who is this man for you?

Finally, each of us must decide about the one who calms the wind and stills the sea—this one who comes to us across the waves and says, "Be of good cheer. It is I. Be not afraid!"

BARTIMAEUS AND THE DISCOURAGEMENT COMMITTEE

Mark 10:46-5

Have you ever felt called to do something or be something, and everyone around you seemed to be telling you that what you wanted to do was impossible or that you should not want to do that? If you open your heart and your mind to the leading of the Holy Spirit and seek to be obedient to where the Holy Spirit is leading you, I will guarantee you that you will encounter many folk who will do all that they can to discourage you in what you are doing. These people are members of what I call the Devil's discouragement committee. We often meet them in our homes, in our families, in our marriage, in the places where we go to school or work, and frequently we meet them in the church. This morning I want to talk with you for a little while about this discouragement committee, how you can recognize it, who is chairman of it, how you may intentionally or unintentionally become a member of it, and what God has done to keep us from being defeated by it.

The passage of scripture that I read from the gospel of Mark just a moment ago is about a man named Bartimaeus and his encounter with a discouragement committee a long time ago. We find the story in Mark 10:46-52. I invite you to look at this with me as we think together about this important issue.

Mark tells us that Jesus and his disciples had come to Jericho on their way to Jerusalem. Jericho is a city in the Jordan Valley about twenty miles northeast of Jerusalem. It is also a city where God acted in a mighty way years before, in the Old Testament. We read about Jericho in the book of Joshua. It was a city that was hostile to the people of God who were being led by Joshua. Moses had died. The people had entered the land that God had promised to give them, and as they moved into that land they came to the city of Jericho. Joshua sent two spies into the city to find out what was there. While there, the spies were hidden and sheltered by a woman named Rahab who was a prostitute. She protected them from the king of Jericho who sought to kill them, and then helped them to escape. Jericho was a great walled city and there seemed no way to take it, but God sent a messenger to Joshua and told him that God had given the city into his hands. And you know the rest of the story. How Joshua followed God's direction and took his soldiers and seven priests and the ark of the covenant and marched around the city once each day for six days, and on the seventh day they marched around the city seven times and blew their trumpets seven times. And the walls of Jericho fell down and they took the city, and the only people who were saved were Rahab and her relatives.

So Jericho was not just a city along the way to Jerusalem. It was city where God had performed a mighty work and had used as his instrument a most unlikely person to help, Rahab the prostitute. Mark tells us that Jesus is passing through Jericho on his way to Jerusalem. God's people are on the march again. And while they are leaving Jericho they pass by a man named Bartimaeus. He is also a very unlikely person to be used to show the power of God. He is poor. He is a beggar who sits by the side of the road and lives on whatever others will give him. Bartimaeus is a nobody. He is the first-century equivalent of a street person, and to make matters worse, he is blind.

We do not know how, but Bartimacus must have heard about Jesus, for when he hears that he is passing by, he calls out to him. "Jesus of Nazareth, Son of David, have mercy on me!" A naked cry for help. A pitiful, prayerful cry from someone who literally had no power. And it is when Bartimaeus cried out that he met the discouragement committee.

Look at what the scripture tells us in verse 48. "And many rebuked him, telling him to be silent." *Shut up, Bartimaeus—you're just a blind beggar and nothing can be done for you. Nobody wants to be bothered with your cries for help. Be quiet.* The wisdom of the discouragement committee.

You've heard that voice when someone or something in you has said that things can't change in your life, or in your family, or in your marriage. *Just make the best of a bad situation. Don't make a spectacle of yourself.* We hear that voice speaking in the land when we are told to quit talking about the needs of the poor or the broken. *We have always had the poor with us.* We hear it counsel us not to be naive about peace—*there have always been wars and rumors of wars. Be realistic.*

What can one person do, or what can this church do? The discouragement committee comes to church at times and says, *We can't really make a difference in our neighborhood or our city or our nation or the world.* You hear the voice of the discouragement committee in your ear when you have tried and tried to overcome a bad habit or change the direction or your life and the voice says, *Why don't you just give up. You've always been a loser and you will always be a loser.* Have you ever heard that voice? I have. I have heard it in my ear from within. I have heard it in the church. I have heard it in this city. I hear it every day and so do you. There are times that we are even members of that committee.

Whose committee is it? Who is chairman of the discouragement committee? Look back at Mark 8:31-33. We thought about that passage several weeks ago. Jesus tells his disciples that he is going down to Jerusalem and there he will be rejected by the scribes and the priests and be killed, and on the third day he will rise from the dead. And guess who shows up as the spokesperson for the discouragement committee? Peter. Peter takes Jesus aside and begins to rebuke him. In Matthew 16:22 we are told that Peter said to Jesus, "God forbid it, Lord. This must never happen to you." And what does Jesus say? He calls Peter Satan. Who is chairman of the discouragement committee? The prince of darkness. The evil one. The one that the Bible calls a liar and a thief.

There are many examples of the work of this committee in the Old Testament. The discouragement committee was at work in a group of spies who came back after going in to look at the land that God had promised to the children of Israel, and reported that it was impossible to take the land. The people were too strong. The way was too difficult. And the people listened to the discouragement committee and wished they were back in Egypt. When the people of God came back from the Babylonian captivity and, under the leadership of Ezra, set out to rebuild the temple, the scripture tells us that the people of the land, those who had been left behind, discouraged the people and they were afraid to build. When God appeared to Moses in the wilderness in the burning bush and instructed Moses to go up to Egypt and say to Pharaoh, "Let my people go," Moses heard the voice of discouragement in his ear and said to God, "Suppose the people won't listen to me. I am not an eloquent person. I am slow of speech and slow of tongue."

How do we recognize the discouragement committee? It is any group or any person that tells us that we cannot or should not do the things that God is calling us to do. It is any group or any person who tells us not to trust God or the promises of God, that tells us to believe that nothing can be done to transform me or you or the world.

Bartimaeus heard the voice of discouragement, but look what he did. He refused to be silenced by it. The scripture tells us that he continued to cry out. And when he did this, when he cried out with persistence and refused to listen to the voice of the discouragers, Jesus listened to him. And Jesus stopped and said, "Call him!" And suddenly the discouragement committee becomes the encouragement committee. They turn to Bartimaeus and say, "Take heart, rise, he is calling you." Now *that* is the voice of light and not of darkness. And Bartimaeus comes to Jesus and Jesus asks him the same question he asked James and John: "What do you want me to do for you?" And Bartimaeus does not say, "Let me be the greatest in the kingdom." He does not say, "Let me sit on your right hand when you come in your power." He asks for the very thing that we should ask for. He says, "Master, let me receive my sight. Master, cure my blindness."

Now isn't that what we should be asking Jesus to do for us? Lord, let me receive my sight. Cure my blindness. Cure me of believing that how it is, is the only way it can ever be. Cure me of falling prey to the discouragers of the world. Cure me from looking at people in my family, or in my school or at my work or on the street, with the eyes of the world, and not with the eyes of Jesus. "Master, let me receive my sight."

The voices of discouragement are all around us. Pray that God will deliver you from being seduced by the prince of darkness into becoming a member of his discouragement committee. Pray that God will deliver us from being seduced by the prince of darkness into speaking words of despair in a world that desperately needs to hear of hope.

How do we keep from being defeated by the discouragers of the world? We do what Bartimaeus did. We continue to cry out. We refuse to listen to those who would silence or discourage us. We

172

come to God with a passion to receive from God our sight and we pray persistently to him. And when the Lord hears us and turns to us and asks, "What do you want me to do for you?" we ask him to give us what we need—new vision and the capacity to follow Jesus along the way. And that is what Bartimaeus did when he received his sight. Mark tells us that he followed Jesus along the way.

What has God done to rescue us from the discouragers of the world? John 3:16 put it clearly and succinctly. "For God so loved the world that he sent his only son that whosoever believes on him should not perish, but have eternal life." Jesus Christ came for you. He died for you. He shed his blood for you. He did this so that you can appear before God on the Day of Judgment, clothed not in the filthy rags of your own mistakes and failures, but clothed in the righteousness of Jesus Christ. Do you believe that? Or do you listen to the discouragement committee that says, "That can't be true. That's a notion out of the dark ages. This is all there is and there isn't any more. The way you are is the way you will always be." Whose voice is that? It is the voice of the evil one who is a liar and a thief.

If you are here today and you have surrendered to some voice of discouragement about yourself or about your marriage or family or your work or the world, hear this. This Jesus who was crucified, dead, and buried, was raised on the third day and is alive forever more. This Jesus who met Bartimaeus a long time ago on the road out of Jericho, can do more abundantly than you can ask or think. This Jesus can make all things new. He can even make *you* new and different. He can give you your sight, and in his company you can find the power and the courage to follow him along the way.

Years ago I attended a conference at Lake Junaluska, North Carolina. Near the end of the conference an old man got up and told us of how he had become very ill, and how everyone around him was ready to give up on the possibility of his recovery. In fact, they were ready to give him up for dead. But this old man stood before us, strong and vital, and said, "Brothers and sisters, I am standing before you today because God is still in the healing business."

God is still in the healing business. He gave Bartimaeus his sight and he has the power to make all things new. That is the good news of the gospel.

A PROPER ANXIETY

Exodus 32:1-14 Philippians 1:21-27 Matthew 6:24-34

"When the people saw that Moses delayed to come down from the mountain, the people gathered themselves together to Aaron and they said to him, 'Up, make us gods who shall go before us. As for this Moses, the man who brought us out of the land of Egypt, we do not know what has become of him.'"

Up, make us gods who shall go before us. What could have led this people to make this bizarre request? These people had come so far and seen so much. It was in their midst that a man named Moses had appeared and said he was an agent of God sent to say to Pharaoh, "Let my people go!" They had seen the plagues in Egypt that had brought Pharaoh to his knees. They saw the work of the angel of death that had passed over their homes and touched instead the houses of their oppressors, striking dead the firstborn in every Egyptian family. They had watched in wonder as the waters of the Red Sea parted. They had walked out of Egypt on dry land. Manna had fallen from heaven to give them their daily bread. When they became thirsty, water had sprung forth from a rock. They had come so far, and they had seen so much.

These events were not simply memories unauthenticated by personal experience and told to them by some ancient grandmother. These people who came to Aaron and said, "Up, make us gods who will go before us," had been there. They had seen it with their own eyes. They had felt the mud between their toes as they walked where the waters of the Red Sea had recently flowed. If there were ever a people who should have known better and done better, it was this liberated band of former slaves. Thus, it is with surprise and shock that we read these words in the 32nd chapter of Exodus. "Up, make us gods who shall go before us. As for this man Moses, we do not know what has become of him."

Deep in the southern tip of the Sinai, deep in the wilderness, far from slavery but even further from the promised land, these descendants of Israel recently liberated from the taskmasters of

Egypt suddenly found themselves slaves to a new master. It was not external pressure that captured their hearts and cut the nerve of their freedom. Scripture does not suggest that Satan slipped in among them incognito, whispering in their ears to build a golden calf. Nor were they coerced by a foreign power or commanded by a conquering king to do such a thing. No outside agent would bear the burden of responsibility for their action. It was on their own initiative that they came to Aaron and pleaded, asked, commanded that he build them something that they could see, touch, and give their freedom to.

And what was the rationale for their action? What explanations would they have offered if they had been asked to justify this act? Was it because they wanted to be like the Egyptians whose land was populated with idols and seemed to be the pinnacle of success? Was it because they wanted to be like the people that they had seen along the way who worshipped all manner of graven images? Was it because they feared that Moses had deserted them, or forgotten them, or perhaps was even dead, and they would now be forced to survive with no one to lead them? Surely they must have felt all of those things. But behind all of these things was a common feeling that led them to offer up all that they were and all that they had been called to be, in exchange for a golden calf. They were *anxious*.

Deep in the Sinai, liberated from their captors, headed toward possibility and newness, they could not stand the burden of their freedom. Soren Kierkegaard said: "Anxiety is the dizziness of freedom." Dostoyevsky's Grand Inquisitor knew this when he said, "Nothing has ever been more insupportable for a man and a human society than freedom. Man is tormented by no greater anxiety than to find someone to whom he can hand over the gift of freedom." Deep in the Sinai, the descendants of Israel felt the anxiety of their freedom, and sought to rid themselves of it by surrendering it to an idol of their own creation.

They did not trust God. They did not trust Moses. They did not trust themselves. They were anxious about their future, anxious about their safety, anxious about their differentness, anxious about their freedom. They came to Aaron and said to him, "Free us from our anxiety. Give us something tangible, easy, and unambiguous to do."

It was not just the people who were anxious. Aaron was also anxious. He had been elected or appointed an elder of these people. Entrusted with their care, told to be responsible for their leadership and their guidance, he was anxious about their approval. He wanted them to like him. His congregation came to him and said, "Freedom makes us dizzy. Being different makes us uncomfortable. Having to take responsibility for our future and our calling makes us frightened. Make us feel better, Brother Aaron. Up, make us gods who will go before us. As for Moses, we do not know what happened to him." And Aaron gave them what they wanted. He gave them a building program. They built a golden calf. For a deeper, more profound anxiety about duty and responsibility and future and faithfulness, they substituted an anxiety about a local project, which they could manage and control and which made them like everyone else. They wanted a project that would reduce the different-ness between them and their pagan neighbors. And in the process, they exchanged their freedom for a new kind of slavery.

Years ago, Sigmund Freud said that the central problem of mental illness is anxiety. Years before Sigmund Freud, another Jew, Jesus of Nazareth, said that anxiety is the central problem of spiritual illness. Of all the things that Jesus talked about, warnings about caring about the wrong things frequently took center stage. Visiting his friends Mary and Martha, he found Martha worried in his presence about the meal, about the house, about how she looked, about how things were going. He spoke words to her that he might easily have said to any of us. "Martha, you are anxious about many things. One thing is needful." In his Sermon on the Mount he told his hearers not to be anxious about food or drink or clothing. When his disciples came to him and said, "Teach us how to pray properly," he gave them a prayer that contained instructions about proper caring. "Give us this day our daily bread." You are to address God as "Our Father" and to remember that he knows your needs and cares for you.

But is it not true that most of us are like the Israelites who were driven by lesser anxieties in the wilderness to the worship of golden calves? We, too, have passed through waters in our baptism. We have heard the stories. We have made our profession of faith. We have the church, the law, and the sacraments. We know better. We have been set free to be children of God, but the truth is that most of us have traded away the anxiety that accompanies that kind of awful freedom for anxiety about things that are not worthy of us.

Anxious about what we shall eat, about what we shall wear or the kind of car we drive or the way our houses look, we become slaves of our jobs or of our office. We are unavailable to do anything but serve this idol that promises to give us all of the things that we want with all our hearts. Anxious about our professional success and prestige, we become slaves to the opinions of our peers. Anxious about our need to be liked and not to be ostracized in our local community, we too quickly agree with every local, provincial, half-witted opinion and prejudice in the hope that all will speak well of us. And if you are a preacher worrying about all the wrong things, you may even have a coronary in the noontime of your life. "Martha," Jesus said, "you are worried and troubled about many things. One thing is needful."

We have become captives of cheap anxieties about how we look, about how much we make, about our degrees, about whether our article or book will be published or if we will get a good job. We give up the lives of freedom we have been given and lose them in pursuit of idols.

It is not hard to find me standing in a crowd before Aaron that day. It's probably not hard for you to find yourself standing there, saying to some modern Aaron, "Give me something easy to be anxious about. Let us be anxious about money, about salary, about buildings, about church growth or about how we look, or about militarism or nationalism or inflation, or the Dow Jones average, or the cost of living. Give us something to be anxious about." Certainly some of these things represent normal and appropriate concerns. But our gospel tells us that none of them should occupy the center stage in our lives. The question we should ask and the question that our new officers should ask is this: "Is there something about which we should be properly anxious?"

Years ago, Carlyle Marney helped me with this when he said, "We should be anxious about the Kingdom of God." You can be properly anxious about that. To be human, to be here in God's image, to be entrusted with God's creation, means that we are entitled to be anxious and concerned about the things that God is anxious and concerned about. If I read the Scriptures with any understanding at all, it appears to me that God is concerned about the well-being of his creation. He entrusted it to us. He said, "Care for it. Be concerned about it. Be sure that it is O.K." And when Jesus came, he said, "I have come to preach good news to the poor and release to the captives." The question that we should be asking about ourselves and about our church is not how much money do we have or how well are we doing. One question that must finally be asked is, "Are we good news to the poor?" Unless we are anxious about the Kingdom of God, we do not have the right to call ourselves a church. Our church should help us to have and maintain a proper anxiety about the things of God. That's what your officers should be concerned about. That's what your pastor should be concerned about. That's what your Sunday School classes should be concerned about. That's what the Women of the Church should be concerned about. That's what all of the committees of the church should be concerned about: the things of God. That's what we ought to be anxious about. Those are proper anxieties for the church.

We need to remember that the real work of the church cannot be counted and reduced to statistics. The numbers of people who show up cannot measure it, or who do not show up, or how much money we take in or do not take in. Church happens when people become properly anxious about the Kingdom of God and act on the basis of that anxiety. If that proper anxiety is not present, then no matter what else we may be, it is doubtful that we are being what we should be.

"Do not be anxious," Jesus said, "about what you will eat, about what you will wear, about what you will put on." Begin your prayers with "Our Father," who knows your needs and cares for you. Seek first, be anxious about, the Kingdom of God, and all of the other things you need will be there as well.

HEALING ON THE HIGHWAY

Luke 17:11-19

Well, what do you think about this little story that is contained in eight brief verses of scripture about Jesus and the lepers? What does such a story have to do with the life that you and I lead from Sunday to Sunday? What in God's name could it have to do with you and with me?

Jesus is on the road somewhere between Samaria and Galilee. Passing through an unnamed village, he encounters ten lepers. They were huddled together, away from anyone else, because it was against the law for them to have contact with folk whose skin was clean. In spite of their isolation, they had somehow heard of Jesus. They had heard he was a healer. And as he was passing by, they cried out for his mercy. To this naked cry for mercy Jesus responds with sternness. There is no pastoral care. There is no word of comfort or understanding or empathy. He simply says to them, "Go! Go and show yourselves to the priests." Go and present yourselves to the Public Health officials of that day. No promise or prescription. Just a command: Go! And in the New English version of the Bible it says simply that "while they were on their way they were healed."

Is this really an irrelevant word from the gospel for all of us whose skin is clean? Or could it be that this story is about something that transcends leprosy and goes far beyond some unnamed village between Samaria and Galilee? Is there something in this story about my story and about your story and about the stories of folk we meet along the way? Where are the lepers today? Is there something in me that needs to be healed because it has left me crippled and isolated? I believe that in this little story of Jesus and the lepers, there is a word for us about healing, about trust, and about what can happen to us and through us.

Where are the lepers today? They are all around us. You may be one of them. To be a leper is to have something that has isolated you from joy, from hope, from community. It may be a broken heart or a broken dream. It is anything that you feel you should hide from others because you believe that no one would want to see it or know about it or hear about it. It is a grief that will not heal. It is the festering soreness of guilt that can find no forgiveness. It is a secret too awful to be shared with anyone and is kept hidden and isolated. It is a memory that you don't want to remember because it is a memory of abuse or of humiliation from long ago. We pass lepers every day. You may be one of them. I may be one of them.

I met one this week. I do not know her name. I had been to dinner with friends after performing a wedding. I was wearing my clerical collar, so my vocational identity was no secret. Walking out of the restaurant, she stood with a group. As I passed by she spoke to me. I stopped. "Do I know you?" I asked.

"I am in your church," she responded. I thought she was a member of First (Scots). She thought I was an Episcopal priest.

"I'm an Episcopalian. I'm from Atlanta. Can I ask you something? Have you heard of Campus Crusade for Christ?"

"I have," I responded.

"My son was in Campus Crusade. He became a Christian with Campus Crusade. He went and told others about his Jesus. He loved Jesus and gave his life to him. But last February my son was killed. A drunk driver killed him and his girlfriend. He was eighteen. He was my only son. He was my only child. Where is my son now? Is my son all right now? Is my boy all right?" And the tears ran down her face.

Her friends stood at a distance talking to one another. Standing on a sidewalk on East Bay Street, I heard a naked cry for help!

"Do you have a priest that you can talk to?" I asked her.

" No. He is new. He does not know me."

"Can you talk to your husband?"

"No. I am trying to be strong for him." And the tears ran down her face.

At that point her husband came back to get her. "Your wife is in great pain," I said. "You must find someone who can see the pain and hear the pain." And then she was gone. Her grief had found no healing. It had isolated her from her church. It was isolating her from her husband. And in front of a restaurant in a town far from home, she had told her story to a stranger. A divine appointment between two lepers.

Where are the lepers? We pass them on the street. They work with us. They may live with us. You may be sitting beside one in this place. You may be one of them.

"On the way . . . between Samaria and Galilee as he entered a village, he met ten lepers who stood at a distance and lifted up their voices and said, 'Jesus, Master, have mercy on me.'"

There is much in this story that can guide us. There is much in this story that is cause for hope. There is much in this story that shows us what we need to do, if we are to be healed.

The first thing that we notice in this story that these ten lepers were very clear about their need to be healed. They confessed that need. They came to Jesus and cried out for healing. In order to be healed, you must know and confess your need for healing. And that is why many folk never experience any healing. They have used their affluence and their success to hide their need for healing from themselves and from others. They sit in pews on Sunday with no cry for wholeness and no recognition of a need for the redeeming love of Jesus Christ. The Bible says, "If we say we have no sin, we deceive ourselves and the truth is not in us; but if we confess our sins"—if we come to God and say, *I am a sinner. I am broken. I need to be healed*—"God is faithful and just and will forgive our sins and will cleanse us from all unrighteousness." But in order to receive it, we must acknowledge we need it. If you don't ask, you may not receive.

How many of us live in spiritual denial while some spiritual leprosy eats away at our soul, and we do not see the symptoms until it is almost too late? A man came to see a counselor, brought by his wife. They were separated. She cried out for help. The man was on crutches. He had fallen out of a tree while he was drunk and had broken both legs and his pelvis. He had lost his license for driving under the influence. He had lost his job for coming to work drunk. His wife had left him because he was wasting what money they had on booze. "How long have you had a problem with alcohol?" the counselor asked. The man responded, "I don't have a problem. I'm doing just fine by myself."

You don't get better until you acknowledge you need to be healed. The lepers knew they had a problem.

Years ago a woman called me to see about getting married. She was not a member of the congregation. I told her that she needed to come and see me for premarital counseling. Her response: "I don't need no pre-marriage counseling. I've been married four times."

The lepers knew they had a problem. They were a long way past denial. It was their recognition of their need and their cry for help that was the first step on the journey toward healing.

But just knowing you have a problem is not enough. These folk asked for help. They reached out. They were not resigned to staying sick. They refused to be still just because crying out might upset someone. They were even willing to make a public spectacle of themselves in order to get help. They cried out. But they didn't just cry out to the sky. They cried out to Jesus. They came and cried out to one that had come to seek and to save the lost. They came to one that they believed could help, and asked for help. And then they did what they were told to do. They didn't argue with the directions. They followed the directions that they received. And on the way, an amazing thing happens. On the way they were made clean.

I could give you a hundred examples of folk who have followed the call and of folk who have not. A couple struggling with a broken marriage are encouraged by a friend to seek help. They refuse. They are too ashamed and the festering sore of estrangement grows worse, until one day the marriage dies. I met a person once who told me that he was a member of a particular church. "Do you go?" I asked. "No," was the reply. "I haven't gone since my father died." How long ago did your father die? "He died twenty years ago, and I am afraid if I go back to church I will cry." What the person was saying was, "I will keep my grief hidden—and in the process I will keep my grief, even if it isolates me from the family of faith."

182

Is something in you crying out to be healed? Is there something in you that is like a pain that never leaves? What to do? Do what you are told to do or led to do. Go and show yourself to a priest: go and show your hurt to someone who can mediate the love and the grace of God to you—go and present yourself to another person who is loving and who knows the Lord. It may be anyone, for we believe in the priesthood of all believers. And along the way, you will be made whole.

One final word. Jesus says to us, "As the Father has sent me, so send I you." We are in the world as living reminders of the love and the grace and the mercy of God. Let us pray that God will give us eyes to see the lepers and not be afraid to call them to the journey that leads to healing. Let us pray that God will give us eyes to see our own leprosy and find the courage to go on the journey, even when at the outset it may seem to make no sense and despair is like a great weight about our necks. The miracle of healing happens gradually, as we are on the way.

The truth is that life is lived on the basis of enough light for the next step. That is about all we are ever given. In spite of all of our planning, all of our need to be in control, it is the unexpected things that happen that change the whole picture. Often it is not in *our* appointments that we find the healing we need, but it is in the divine appointments when some unexpected person shows up in our lives and calls us to go on a journey that will lead to wholeness. Perhaps my encounter with the woman who told me of her grief about her son was, in some strange way, an answer to some of her prayers for healing and relief. I do not know. I did not plan to meet her nor did she plan to meet me. It was a divine appointment. Our paths crossed and she cried out for healing. And I told her to find someone you can talk to. Find a priest. Show him or her your wounds and you will be made whole.

The real sign of God working in our lives is that we will be led in a way we did not plan to go, and on the way we will be made clean.

Dr. Eichelberger's heart disease resulted in his early retirement in 1996. On his last Sunday as the senior pastor of First (Scots) Presbyterian Church, he delivered this farewell sermon.

REFLECTIONS ON LEAVING

Ecclesiastes 3:1-14   Revelation 21:1-6   Luke 12:22-31

I come to this moment feeling a little like the man who had written on his tombstone, "I Knew This Was Going to Happen." I knew that this would happen eventually. I did not expect it to have happened quite this soon, but things often get over with before we are finished. What is really amazing to me is how much we have accomplished in a rather short period of time. It has been good to be here, and it is hard to leave.

As I was reflecting on leaving, I found my mind taking me back to an event that happened about fifteen years ago. The event was the selling of my parent's house. My parents had built it when they were married, and it was the house I was brought home to when I was born. When I thought about home, I thought about this house. Several years prior to this event my mother, who was then a widow, had moved to the Presbyterian Home in Clinton, South Carolina. The house was left vacant. We were reluctant to sell it for a variety of reasons, but finally we all agreed that it should be done. A part of the process was to divide the furniture up and give to various members of the family the things they wanted. So one day in May I drove alone to Clinton from Asheville, North Carolina, where we were living at the time.

I arrived at the house with my old station wagon and a trailer, and I backed into the driveway. There was no one there. I used the key that my brother had sent me and opened the door and went in to locate the few things that were left there that were supposed to be mine. I began to carry the pieces of furniture out to the trailer. Suddenly it struck me that I had never seen the house without furniture in it. I carried a couple of more pieces out, and then suddenly and without warning I was overcome with a terrible sense of sadness. I sat down on the tailgate of the trailer, and I began to cry.

I was puzzled by the intensity of my feelings. Why was I so sad? What I was doing was right and perfectly logical. But then I realized that my grief was about something of profound significance that was coming to an end. I was standing in the face of that reality in a way that was inescapable. I walked back into the house and stood in the living room and remembered where all the Christmas trees had been. I walked into what had been my bedroom and remembered nights lying there wondering what I might be when I grew up. I remembered sitting with my father in the kitchen late in the day after we had been fishing together. I remembered long afternoons talking with my mother about books and plays. I remembered my brother as a small boy and my sisters growing up. But the thing that I was grieving for was not any particular memory, but for the fact that a large piece of my life was now over. The chapter about being a family in that house was over, and the reality of that broke over me like a huge wave and took charge of me for a little while. It reminded me again of how parts of your life come to an end. Parts of our life come to an end before we are finished, before all the unfinished business is worked out, before all the "I love you's" have been said, and all the "I'm sorry's" have been heard, and all the "I forgive you's" have been spoken. This was it. It was over, and the life we had shared there in that place as a family was now history. Some of it had been wonderful, and some of it had been painful. Some of it I could celebrate, and some of it left me feeling sad because everything had not been fully resolved.

Driving back home that day I remembered the words from one of my favorite hymns: "Time, like an ever-rolling stream, bears all its sons away." Things come to an end. Time bears all its sons and daughters away. Life gets finished before we are ready for it to be finished.

I thought about that memory recently while I was reflecting on my leaving here. This past week, after a Session meeting was over, I walked around the church for a little while by myself. I remembered the Advent services and the Easter services, the weddings, the funerals, the baptisms. I remembered people we had said hello to and people we had said goodbye to. I felt blessed and grateful and sad all at the same time.

I suppose every time we come up against something like this, and I know we all have had similar experiences, we are reminded of our own mortality and the temporariness of life.

What do we do when we have experiences like this? Do we build walls around us to avoid any pain of parting in the future? Do we shut our feelings down and pretend that nothing really touches us? Is there any good news from the Lord that will sustain us in joy and in sorrow, in these experiences that are as common to you as they are to me?

I think there is, and I think that the three lessons that were read today can provide us with some direction and wisdom as we seek to live creatively and hopefully in the midst of changes.

First, we need to face the truth about change. Change is neither bad nor good. It is inevitable. As long as you are alive, you are changing. In fact, the essence of life is change. The only way to stop changing is to die. The book of Ecclesiastes tells us that there is a time for beginnings and endings. There is an order to things that are a part of our living. There is a time to be born and a time to die, a time to weep and a time to laugh, a time to keep and a time to cast away. Living involves changing. If a baby never changed, that baby would never grow up. There are moments in life about which we would like to say, "Stay a little while," but the good moments pass and drift away, as do the difficult moments. There is a time to be a child, a time to be an adolescent, and a time to be an adult. There is a time to prepare for work, a time to work, and a time to retire. Perhaps the only thing that does not change is change itself. I am sorry that our time together is concluding, but it has been wonderful. The memories cannot be taken away. The only way that I could have avoided this moment of sadness would have been to have never known you or been with you, and I wouldn't have missed that for the world. This church has been here for a long time and it will be here for a long time in the future. There have been great changes in the past, and there will be changes in the future. A wise friend of mine once said that with every loss there is a gain and with every gain there is a loss. I believe that is true.

And then if we going to live creatively with all the changes of life we should remember that we are not alone. God is with us.

God knows you and loves you. God loves this church. The word for us in this time of transition is to "be not afraid." Jesus said to his disciples and to folk who came to hear him, in the twelfth chapter of Luke, "Do not be anxious about your life." Do not be worried. Do not be afraid. God will take care of you. And we know, as the apostle Paul knew, that nothing can separate us from the love of God. I go out from this place truly not knowing where I am to go and what I am to do, but I go knowing that the God who called Abraham to go on a journey will be with me in all of my tomorrows. And so will that God be with you. He will be with you in whatever journey you are on. And many of you *are* on a journey. It may be a journey through grief, or a journey through sickness, or a journey through broken hopes and broken dreams. Each day we continue the journey, never sure what the day will bring. One man was asked if he could give a description of what he thought heaven was like. He said, "Yes, heaven is where all the rules are fair and there will be good surprises." In the proximate future all the rules will probably not be fair and there will be painful and difficult surprises, but that is not the entire story. We Christians know the rest of the story. We know that there is no need to be anxious or afraid in the changes of life. We may not know what the future holds, but we know who holds the future.

And finally, in the midst of change we must live our lives not in the light of the evidence, but in the light of the promises of God. It takes no great creativity or deep searching to gather enough evidence to say that there is no God. It is not hard to find evidence to support the conclusion reached by the poet who wrote, "Men must die and women must weep and the sooner it's over the sooner we sleep." On the island of Patmos, John, who was a prisoner in exile with no prospects for any good future, had a vision. He recorded it in the twenty-first chapter of Revelation when he said, "I saw a new heaven and a new earth, for the old had passed away." And in that day God will be with us, and he will wipe away every tear, and there will be no more death, or mourning, or crying, or pain, or cancer, or AIDS, or heart disease, or deadly illnesses that tear our children and our loved ones from our arms, and there will be no more parting. The old will have passed away, and in this final, great change, the new will have come because our God is a God who makes all things new.

So today I say goodbye to you as your pastor. I want to thank you for your love, for your gracious acceptance of me and my family, for your support and prayers when I was sick, for giving me the privilege of being your pastor, and for the opportunity of sharing our life and time for a while. Many of you have told me how much I have meant to this church. If I have made a difference while I was here, I am grateful, but give God the glory. You have meant more to me than I could possibly have meant to you.

When Jules Anderson, chairman of the pulpit nominating committee that brought my name to this congregation, talked to me about coming here, I asked him what the church was looking for. He didn't say a good preacher or a good counselor, or a good administrator. Rather, he said, "We want someone who will love us and someone whom we can love." Let me assure you that you have done your part for me and for Priscilla. We have tried to do that for you. I feel that I am one of the most fortunate people in the world today because I am concluding my active parish ministry career in the midst of a vital, growing, exciting congregation, and people who have blessed me in so many ways surround me. I wish I could have stayed a little longer, but that was not to be. I will miss you. I will miss preaching in this pulpit. I will miss my relationship with the outstanding staff of this church. I will miss the outstanding music given by Larry and the choir; I will miss being the pastor of such a gracious and loving congregation. But there is a time to say hello and a time to say goodbye—a time to begin and a time to stop. You will always be with me. It's been wonderful to be here. I wouldn't have missed it for the world. God bless you, First (Scots) Presbyterian Church. God bless us one and all.

About The Author

Hugh Lee Eichelberger, Jr. was born in 1934 in Clinton, South Carolina, attended local schools, then graduated from the McCallie School in Chattanooga, TN. He attended Clemson University on a football scholarship before transferring to Presbyterian College in Clinton, where he graduated with a major in English. He and Priscilla Ruth Dickson, of Anderson, SC, married in 1955. He served as a lieutenant in the Army's anti-aircraft artillery in Fort Bliss, Texas, then taught and coached football at McCallie School before earning a Master of Divinity degree from Columbia Theological Seminary in Atlanta; he also served as a chaplain at Grady Memorial Hospital in Atlanta. In addition to serving churches in North Carolina, Virginia, South Carolina, and Florida, he served for two years on the national staff of the Presbyterian Church, US. He later earned his Doctor of Ministry degree in counseling from Columbia Seminary. From 1991 to 1996, he was the senior pastor at First (Scots) Presbyterian Church in Charleston, SC, and preached all the sermons in this book from that pulpit.

As a pastoral counselor, Dr. Eichelberger was a Clinical Member of the American Association of Marriage and Family Counselors, and was a Fellow and member of the national Board of the American Association of Pastoral Counselors; he also served as national president of the Academy of Parish Clergy. During a pastorate in Richmond, Virginia, he was an adjunct member of the faculty of Union Theological Seminary and the Virginia Institute for Pastoral Care. In 1986 he was named a Fellow at the College of Preachers at the National Cathedral in Washington.

While in Charleston, Dr. Eichelberger presented several sermons on "The Protestant Hour" (now known as "Day1"), an international, ecumenically-sponsored radio broadcast. He also wrote a column on marriage and family issues for the Charleston *Post and Courier*. Other writings by Dr. Eichelberger have appeared in *The Journal of Pastoral Care*, *The Presbyterian Survey*, *Monday Morning*, and *Lectionary Homiletics*. Hugh and Priscilla Eichelberger have retired to a mountaintop home in western North Carolina, where they enjoy volunteering, beekeeping, reading and writing. In 2005 their four children and eight grandchildren gathered to celebrate the couple's fiftieth wedding anniversary. Dr. Eichelberger now writes an occasional column in the *Tryon Daily Bulletin* entitled "From the Top of the Mountain."

Hugh Eichelberger on a recent visit to Mepkin Abbey in Moncks Corner, SC

Audio recordings of some of the sermons in this book may be heard online. Visit http://distanttrumpet.blogspot.com/ to learn more and to contact the author.